Dedication

To my mother, Homesanith, and to the
memory of my grandmother, Sika.

"Sai mae nam is a saying Thais know to mean nurturing, flowing like the mother rivers which bring sustenance and life."

Kham Signavong
Arun Thai Restaurant

kham's
sai mae nam

Photography by Ken Martin

Title: Kham's Sai Mae Nam

Arun Thai Restaurant, 28 Macleay Street, Sydney, Australia

www.arunthai.com.au

National Library of Australia Cataloguing-in-Publication Data

Kham's Sai Mae Nam [includes index]

ISBN: 978-0-9804212-7-99 [hbk]

1. Cookery. 1. Signavong, Kham, 11. Plummer, Alison

Published by True Blue Cockatoo Pty Ltd

www.bluecockatoo.com.au

Authors: Text and recipe copyright © 2009 Khamtane Signavong and Alison Plummer

Photography copyright: © 2009 Ken Martin, Peter Metro, Alison Plummer

Copyright©2009 True Blue Cockatoo

Concept: Ken Martin, Peter Metro, Alison Plummer

Photography: Ken Martin

Design & production: Metro Co

Title: Kham's Sai Mae Nam

Printed by United Production Press, Bangkok, Thailand

First printed 2009 ©True Blue Cockatoo

Khamtane Signavong, Ken Martin, Alison Plummer and Peter Metro have asserted their moral right
to be indentified as the authors of this work.

Every Thai recipe has a history, handed down through generations.

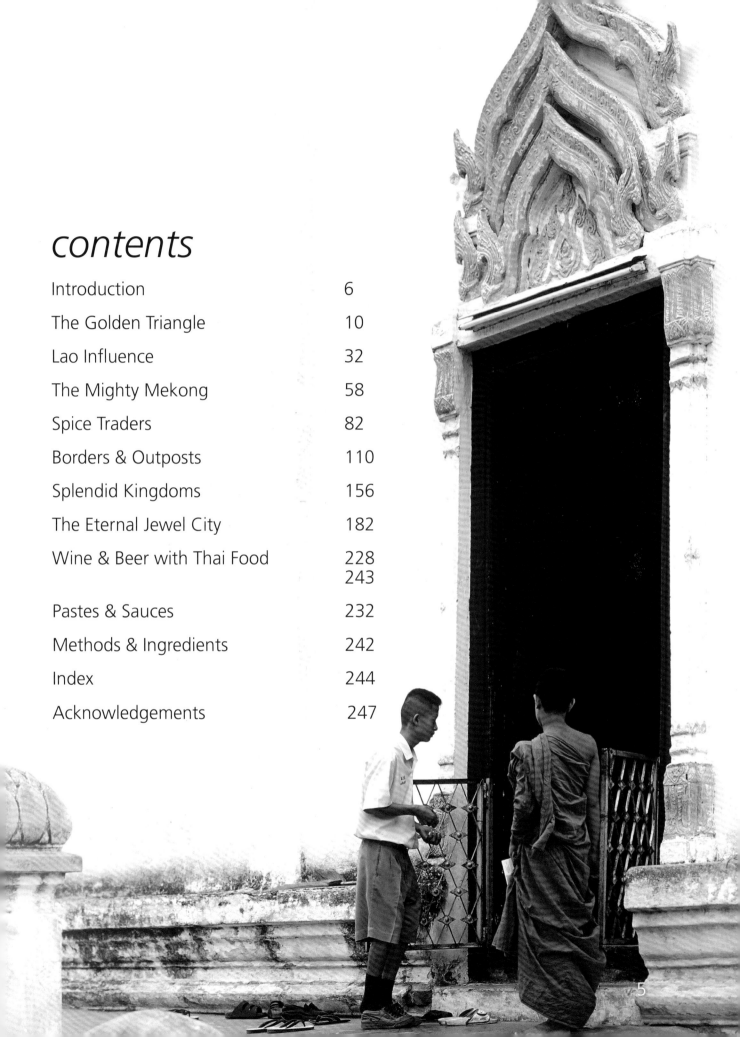

contents

Kham Signavong
Arun Thai Restaurant

"Life is a journey and mine has taken me from my birthplace on the Mekong River to my Arun Thai Restaurant in Sydney, sharing many milestones with my friends and customers along the way."

People often ask me about my birthplace and the origins of the cuisine I serve in my Arun Thai Restaurant. When I tell them that I was born (a Thai) on the Lao side of the Mekong River, they are always fascinated as this mighty river is such a legend that even the mention of the name evokes a sense of adventure and excitement.

I spent my childhood growing up in Savannakhet, Laos and Mukdahan on the Thai side of the river in Isan. For me, and all those who are born along its banks, the 'Mae Kong' is quite simply, home, the source of life giving food for the table, water for rice and crops and allowing travel to other towns and villages in Laos and Thailand. There are many legends and superstitions attached to it such as the great river serpents which are represented in temple architecture and in art.

It was in thinking about the importance of the Mekong River that I looked at Thailand as a whole and how its major river systems (as many as 25) have shaped the country, with the Chao Phraya River basin at its heart, the great food bowl producing great quantities of rice and other crops.

Still vital for agriculture, the rivers were once the lifelines of commerce and the routes by which many influences flowed into Thailand from Tibet, China, Burma (Myanmar), Laos and beyond. Like arteries, the rivers carry water, the life-blood of the land, and sai mae nam is a saying which Thais know to mean flowing like the mother rivers, giving sustenance and life.

As you travel in Thailand you can see the various cultural influences most obviously in the temple architecture and then you discover them in other ways such as the way the local food tastes and is prepared. Looking back over our colourful history, the migration and integration of cultures, it is wonderful to to see how Thailand has maintained a unique identity while gathering from others along the way. Food-wise, Chinese noodles and stir-frying and South American chillies brought by Portuguese traders are outstanding examples!

Most Thais are Theravada Buddhists who revere ancient teachings and the traditional way of conducting our lives which basically does not change. You might say that, while we evolve with the times, we never lose sight of the core values. This flows through everything including cooking where there are ways of doing things to keep a recipe traditional as we were taught by our families. We may present it in a fresh way but the balance of flavours must always be correct.

A contemporary edge, balanced by tradition – a very Thai perspective

Like all Thais, I learned my cooking from my family.

Thais eat freshly cooked food made with ingredients bought the same day
which is as much a part of everyday life now as it was when I was a young boy sent
to shop at the markets for the freshest possible produce and the best seasonal ingredients.

While my roots are in Isan, my restaurant is named after the very beautiful Wat Arun on the banks of
the Chao Phrayha River in Bangkok and we have an extensive menu of Royal Thai Cuisine and regional
dishes reflecting the best of Thailand and the best Australian produce.

My regular customers are very discerning and often just say "what do you have for us today, Kham?"
and are keen to try different dishes. I think about what I have in the kitchen and I might serve,
say, scallops, mud crabs, Wagyu Beef, duck, free-range Barossa chickens, whole snapper or
barramundi, cooking them in a Thai way while allowing the distinctive flavours to be retained.
This allows a contemporary edge balanced by tradition – a very Thai perspective.

Most customers have favourites whether it is a banana flower salad, a prawn or chicken soup,
green curry chicken or noodles such as Pad Thai. If they feel under the weather I might cook
them my grandmother's 'Get Well Soon Soup'.

Returning to Thailand recently I visited Isan, of course, where I met up with family and visited my
grandmother's grave which was a very moving experience. Like all Thais, I learned my cooking
from my family and my grandmother was very special to me. I enjoyed meeting up with cooks
who prepare dishes in the time-honoured way and noting again the fresh flavours of Isan food.

My friends and I then followed the Mekong River to Southern Isan where the Lao influence gives
way to Khmer. We also journeyed to the South for wonderful seafood and flavours so different from
elsewhere in Thailand, rich with spices and flavours from India, Malaysia, Sumatra and beyond. We
travelled North to discover the Burmese and Chinese roots of famous noodle and curry dishes and to
the Central regions where everything comes together in one big fertile food bowl.

Now most ingredients are available all over Thailand, but on my travels I was searching for those who
inspire with dishes that have been prepared for many years by traditional methods. Even in Bangkok,
a city which prides itself on its contemporary edge, I was delighted to find a traditional pastry stall
where irresistible sweet sesame pastries were being made.

My homeland, my family and my customers (who are also like my family) are the inspiration
for this new book and I hope it will also find a broader audience with those who love food,
cooking and hospitality and have a desire to make sure the flavours they produce are as
authentically Thai as possible.

Arun Thai – Thai Select Best Restaurant.

Thai Select

"Thai Select" logo from the Royal Thai Government certifies the authenticity of Thai food ingredients, the high quality of service and the pleasant atmosphere of a Thai restaurant.

Receiving this prestigious award isn't easy, the bar is set high and the guidelines are strict.

Only through dedication and perseverance to a high standard do Thai restaurants worldwide achieve this distinction.

So anywhere in your travels, look for the "Thai Select" Star of approval. This assures you that delicious Thai cuisine is being served in a pleasant atmosphere, with the famous Thai smile. It's not just a meal, it's a journey into Thai cuisine.

The Golden Triangle

This land of river valleys and mountains is remote and beautiful, resonating with the echoes of the past. Divided into the far North and the Northwest, the North of Thailand is a colourful and fascinating blend of cultures, its northernmost point known as the Golden Triangle, where Thailand meets Myanmar and Laos, with China beyond.

Thailand's rich cultural heritage unfolds in its temple styles, murals and carvings.

overland trade routes

Traders from Yunnan in China used trade routes between China, Thailand, Burma and Laos for centuries, but the history of modern Thailand began with the migration of the Tai-Lao speaking people from Southern China around the 10th century. Today many semi-nomadic hill tribe people live in the Far North.

ping river valley

The Ping River rises on the Myanmar border and flows across Thailand to join the Chao Phraya River. The valley is a natural area where traditional life still goes on.

mae hong son

Settled by the Tai Yai people around 1300, this beautiful destination is in a valley surrounded by mountains, with architecture reflecting its Burmese associations, occupied by Tai Yai (Shan) and Karen peoples.

city of temples

Chiang Rai is the gateway to the Golden Triangle and was the original capital before Chiang Mai, a beautiful city which has nearly as many temples as Bangkok, some still featuring the distinctive architecture from the glorious days of the 13th–18th century Lanna Kingdom, meaning land of a million rice fields.

ancient dvaravati chedi

Lamphun was the northernmost city of the Mon kingdom in the Dvaravati period. Wat Chama Thewi has two chedis (spires) built in the 1200s, the last surviving examples of Dvaravati architecture with Buddha images and Hindu gods.

Influences

teak and murals

British traders from Burma established Lampang as a teak centre and many teak houses can be seen here today. Wat Phra That Lampang has a carved façade, murals depicting life in the 16th century and exquisite details such as black lacquered pillars inlaid with gold.

northern specialities

Charcuterie is a local skill with spicy sausages (sai ouar) a speciality. Grilling and simmering are time-honoured cooking methods as well as stir-frying which was introduced by the Chinese.

khao soi noodles

The Chinese influence is seen in dishes such as Khao Soi egg noodles made with beef or chicken in a curry sauce, balanced with the flavours of spring onions and lime.

gaeng hang lay

This Tai Yai favourite is traditional dish originating from Burma (Myanmar), a delicious pork curry made with ginger, tamarind and turmeric.

"Dishes are generally hot and salty with generous use of green chillies, tomatoes, galangal, pepper and Thai aubergines. Conditions here are perfect for mushrooms and leaves from the forests are used for wrapping."

The cool climate of the North creates perfect growing conditions for a rich variety of produce including rice, fruit and vegetables.

gaeng hang lay

slow-cooked hang lay pork curry

600g pork neck,
cut into 2.5-cm cubes

1 tbsp oil

300 ml water

3 whole pickled garlic bulbs

2 medium onions,
peeled and quartered

5 cloves garlic, peeled

50g roasted peanuts

60g fresh ginger,
peeled and julienned
(reserve half for garnish)

5 shallots,
peeled and finely sliced

1½ tbsp tamarind juice

1½ tbsp palm sugar

1½ tbsp fish sauce

1 large chilli,
sliced into 8, lengthways

marinade:

1½ tbsp Hang Lay Curry Paste
(see page 236)

2 tsp ground turmeric

1½ tbsp light soy sauce

½ tbsp dark soy sauce

The Shan people brought Gaeng Hang Lay to the Northern part of Thailand and the recipe here is from a cook named Mae Sri Bua from Mae Hong Son, who wishes to pass on some of her cuisine. She told me that traditionally the Shan people use pork belly but you can also use pork neck which is not as fatty or other meat if you wish.

There are two ways of making Gaeng Hang Lay – in Mae Hon Song it is made with more tamarind juice so it is less sweet than the Chiang Mai version. Gaeng Hang Lay is cooked for various festivals and occasions such as when the boys in the family leave to study or join the army and it is also offered to the Buddhist monks.

Place the pork cubes in a large bowl and mix with the hang lay curry paste, turmeric and dark and light soy sauce.
Place in the fridge to marinate for 2–3 hours.

Heat the oil in a wok, add the marinated pork and cook, stirring until the pork changes colour and begins to brown. Lower the heat, add enough water to just cover the pork, then add the pickled garlic and simmer for 1 hour, stirring occasionally.

Now add the onion, garlic, ginger, shallot, tamarind juice, palm sugar, fish sauce and cook for a further 15–20 minutes or until the pork is tender.

Finally, add the peanuts and chilli, stir and serve garnished with ginger.

*Serves: **4*** *Prep time: **3 hours***
*Cooking time: **1 hour 20-30 mins***

khao soi
chiang mai noodles

600ml coconut milk
(including 3 tbsp cream from the top)

2 tbsp Khao Soi Paste
(see page 236)

350ml chicken stock

1 tbsp curry powder

½ tsp turmeric powder

2 tbsp fish sauce

2 tsp sugar

1 tsp salt

2 stems lemongrass,
finely sliced

160g chicken breast fillet,
sliced into bite-sized pieces

2 litres water

250g egg noodles

100g bean sprouts

1 lime, quartered

2 tbsp fried shallots

handful crispy fried egg noodles

2 shallots,
peeled and finely chopped

2 tbsp pickled vegetables

5 hot chillies,
chopped

handful coriander leaves,
finely chopped

This is the most popular noodle dish from Chiang Mai. More than a hundred years ago, the Jin Hork people sought a new life in the North of Thailand bringing with them one of Thailand's most famous noodle dishes, Khao Soi, made with creamy coconut milk, spices and herbs, served with chicken or beef.

Heat 3 tbsp coconut cream (from the top of the coconut milk) in a pan, add the khao soi paste and stir well until the red oil rises and separates. Add the coconut milk and simmer for 20 minutes.

Pour in the stock, add the curry powder, turmeric, fish sauce, sugar, salt and lemongrass. Turn down the heat and simmer for 30 minutes, then add the chicken and simmer for another 5–6 minutes until cooked.

Bring 2 litres of water to the boil in a large pan, then add the noodles and cook for 1 minute, stirring all the time to prevent them from sticking together. Remove from the heat, drain and divide between four serving bowls. Add the bean sprouts, pour over the sauce and garnish with coriander, fried shallots and the crispy-fried egg noodles.

Serve with lime, shallots, pickled vegetables and chilli on the side.

Serves: **4**   *Prep time:* **45 mins**   *Cooking time:* **1 hour**

larb khua nuer

northern beef larb

50g each of beef tripe,
heart, liver, kidney

2 tsp sea salt

2 tbsp vegetable oil

2 tbsp Larb Khua Paste
(see page 237)

350g beef mince

80ml beef blood jelly

handful coriander leaves,
finely chopped

handful of mint leaves

handful sawtooth leaves
(see page 242)

2 spring onions,
finely chopped

to serve:

lettuce leaves

cucumber slices

snake beans

spring onions

coriander leaves

mint leaves

morning glory

cabbage leaves

sawtooth leaves

wing beans

sticky rice
(see page 242)

Larb from the north is called Larb Khua or Larb Mueang and is very different from the Lao-style larb dishes as it is dry, rich and spicy and traditionally served raw with fresh blood and cooked offal. Sticky rice and fresh vegetables are the accompaniments.

In this recipe everything is cooked so those who don't want their friends and family to think of them as vampires should feel more comfortable.

Place beef offal in a heavy pot and cover with cold water.
Add 1 tsp salt, bring to the boil, then reduce heat and simmer until cooked – about 25 minutes. Remove, drain and slice thinly.

Place the oil in the frying pan add the paste, stir for 2 minutes then add the beef and cook for 3 minutes. Now add the cooked offal and slowly pour in the blood jelly and stir to mix with beef until cooked.

Season with salt to taste, sprinkle with coriander leaves, mint leaves, spring onion and sawtooth leaves, taste and adjust seasoning if necessary, then serve with all the vegetables and sticky rice.

*Serves: **4**   Prep time: **20 mins**   Cooking time: **15 mins***

jin lung

shan slow-cooked meatballs with tomatoes & sesame oil

1kg minced pork

3 eggs

1 litre sesame oil

5 medium-sized tomatoes,
halved

2 onions,
peeled and finely chopped

2–3 tbsp fish sauce,
to taste

1 tsp sugar

2–3 hot chillies,
to taste

3 knobs fresh turmeric,
peeled and finely chopped,

2 kaffir lime leaves,
finely sliced

jin lung chilli paste:

5 hot dried chillies

1 tbsp shrimp paste

banana leaf or foil

8 garlic cloves,
peeled and finely chopped

1tsp salt

1 stem lemongrass,
finely chopped

5 shallots,
peeled and finely chopped

5 galangal rings,
finely chopped

3 coriander roots,
finely chopped

1 tbsp coriander seeds,
toasted

5 kaffir lime leaves,
finely chopped

Make the paste first. Soak the dried chillies in warm water for 30 minutes, remove, drain and de-seed.

Heat the grill, wrap the shrimp paste in banana leaf or foil and grill for about 5 minutes to aromatise. Combine the shrimp paste, garlic, salt, lemongrass, shallot, galangal, coriander and kaffir lime in a large mortar and pound them to the fine paste. Reserve 1½ tbsp to add to the sauce.

Add the pork mince and continue to pound until it is completely mixed with the chilli paste. Transfer to a bowl, crack in the eggs and stir to mix, then roll the mince into 15 balls, each about the size of a golf ball.

Heat the sesame oil in a large pan and fry the meatballs, five at a time. Each batch will take about 5–6 minutes to cook. When cooked, remove and drain on paper towel while the sesame oil cools. Return the meatballs to the cooled oil until ready to serve.

Garnish with kaffir lime and serve with steamed jasmine rice.

Serves: **4**   *Prep time:* **35 mins**
Cooking time: **30 mins**

sai ouar

chiang mai sausages with lemongrass & coriander

2 shallots,
peeled and thinly sliced

4 knobs galangal, finely chopped

4 stems lemongrass,
finely chopped

8 garlic cloves,
peeled and thinly sliced

4 coriander roots

1 tbsp chilli powder

500g pork mince

2 tbsp Red Curry Paste
(see page 238)

4 tsp sea salt

4 tsp caster sugar

8 tsp chopped coriander leaves

1 tsp freshly ground black pepper

1 tsp ground turmeric

4 kaffir lime leaves,
finely sliced

6 sausage casings
(from your butcher)

to serve:

sliced lettuce or cabbage

nuts such as peanuts or cashews

whole chillies

sliced ginger

sticky rice
(see page 242)

Pound the shallots, galangal, lemongrass, garlic and coriander roots to a fine paste using a pestle and mortar.

In a bowl combine the pork mince with the red chilli paste and remaining ingredients (except the sausage casings) and stir to mix well.

Now stuff each casing with the mixture, but do not overfill or they will burst when cooking. You can twist the casings to form balls rather than long sausage shapes, if desired.

Prick the sausages with a fork and barbecue, grill or fry. Serve with nuts, chillies, sliced ginger, lettuce or Chinese cabbage and sticky rice.

Makes: **12**   *Prep time:* **20 mins**   *Cooking time:* **5–8 mins**

nam prik ong

spicy herbed pork dipping sauce

½ tbsp finely chopped galangal

6 dried chillies,
de-seeded and soaked in warm water

5 garlic cloves,
peeled and chopped

3 shallots,
peeled and finely chopped

1 tsp salt

1 tsp shrimp paste

300g minced pork
(or chicken)

12 cherry tomatoes,
halved

2 tbsp cooking oil

100ml water

1–2 tbsp fish sauce,
to taste

½ tbsp white sugar

coriander leaves,
to garnish

to serve:

crisp lettuce leaves
pork crackers

cucumber batons

sliced cabbage

banana blossom

morning glory

steamed snake beans

Thai eggplant

This dipping sauce should be a balance of rich, spicy meat, saltiness from the fish sauce and shrimp paste and sourness from the tomato. The traditional way to eat it is to scoop up sauce and a selection of vegetables into lettuce leaf 'parcels' to eat, or use crispy pork crackers to dip.

Pound the galangal, chillies, garlic, shallots and salt together using a pestle and mortar, stir in the shrimp paste then add the pork and tomatoes and continue to pound.

Heat the oil in a frying pan, add the pork and herb mixture and cook to brown. Turn down the heat and slowly add the water. Cook for a further 10–15 minutes, stirring to prevent sticking, until the dip begins to thicken.

Season with fish sauce and sugar, mix well and taste to check if you need a little more of either, to taste. (As ingredients vary in strength, tasting for balance is very important in Thai cooking.)

Serve the dip in a bowl, garnished with coriander leaves and with lettuce leaves, pork crackers and your selection of fresh and steamed vegetables.

Serves: **4**   *Prep time:* **45 mins**   *Cooking time:* **25 mins**

gai ob fuang

'straw-baked' free-range chicken

1.5 kg whole free-range chicken

Nam Jim Jiew
(spicy dipping sauce,
see page 241)

marinade:

5 garlic cloves,
peeled and finely chopped

1½ tsp white pepper

2 tbsp Mekhong whisky

2 stems lemongrass,
finely chopped

1 tbsp oil

1 tbsp soy sauce

2 tsp sea salt

2 tsp sugar

Back in Thailand I often saw farmers cooking marinated native chicken in drums covered with straw which they burned to cook the chicken. Nowadays most Thais char grill or use gas barbecues but on my recent visit I found a family cooking their chicken with straw in the time-honoured tradition just outside of the city of Lampang. The smoky flavour was second to none.

In a big bowl mix together the ingredients for the marinade. Thoroughly coat the chicken with the marinade and place in the fridge for 3 hours.

Heat the oven to 200°C, place the chicken on a tray and roast for 1 hour, or until cooked. Remove from the oven, chop the chicken into 8 portions then serve with spicy nam jim jiew dipping sauce.

(If you have a Weber-style barbecue or barbecue with char grill you can also cook the chicken that way, adding a rustic, smoky flavour at the end by turning down the heat, adding a handful of straw and closing the lid while the straw smokes.)

Serves: 4   Prep time: 3 hours   Cooking time: 1 hour

The Lao Influence

Sparkling combinations of mint, coriander, chilli, lime and lemon basil flavouring Lao-style larb dishes are signatures of Isan in Northeastern Thailand.

Temples in Northeastern Thailand are influenced by the Lao styles with ornate carving and gilding.

Lao settlers

People from Laos arrived in Isan between the fourteenth and sixteenth centuries and increased their presence from the late eighteenth century escaping from power struggles between Laotian Kingdoms.

Lao-style temples

Intricate carving and gilding are signatures of Lao temples with several different types. The Luang Prabang style is closer to the Lanna style of Northern Thailand with dramatic rooflines that almost reach the ground and featuring carved and gilded gables.

ethnic groups

Of Isan's 20 million or so inhabitants, nearly two million belong to ethnic groups such as Ahue Mon Khmer, Eastern Bru Mon Khmer and Tai Dam, integrated as Thais while speaking their own dialects.

coloured rivers

At Khong Chiam, the muddy red waters of the Mekong River meet the indigo blue of Mun River creating a two-coloured river.

"Isan food is in your face, with plenty of chilli. Mint, spring onion, coriander, lime and lemon basil are used in larbs, the traditional, tangy salads which are a Lao influence. In Isan you can 'larb' anything – and I mean anything – from land, sky or water, as long as it had life!"

Influences

cultural past

Ancient artefacts found at Ban Chiang include pottery believed to be the world's oldest and traces from the Bronze Age show that this was a sophisticated cultural hub in 3000BC.

fresh & spicy

Featuring simple combinations of ingredients, fresh and spicy Isan-style food was once regarded as basic. Now it is regarded as a healthy cuisine which is becoming popular in Thailand as well as elsewhere around the world.

rare mushrooms

The yum hed kon mushroom grows on white ant nests during the monsoon season and is a rare delicacy with a sweet taste.

game from the forests

Once Isan was covered in dense forest, a source of food which influenced the dishes of the region with plentiful wild game and leaves used for wrapping dishes such as spicy sour pork in banana leaves.

papaya salad

Other Isan favourites include BBQ chicken served with tangy papaya salad and pungent pla ra, the fermented fish sauce we love so much, made from pickled mud fish with rice bran and salt.

Rivers support everyday life in the mountainous border regions between Laos and Thailand.

larb pet
isan duck salad

6 sliced galangal rings

250g duck breast,
skin on

100g duck offal

300ml chicken stock

2 tbsp fish sauce

2 tbsp lime juice

½ tsp sugar

½ tsp dried chilli
(to taste)

2 shallots,
peeled and finely chopped

handful mint leaves

1 spring onion,
finely chopped

handful coriander leaves,
finely, chopped

1 tbsp Toasted Rice
(see page 242)

8–10 crispy fried dried chillies,
for garnish

to serve:

lettuce leaves

cucumber slices

snake beans

spring onion tops

sticky rice (see page 242)

Larb is a very rustic dish from Northeastern Thailand which goes very well with sticky rice. It is fresh and sparkling with flavours of chilli, lime, mint, and coriander. It can be made with minced chicken, beef, pork, prawns or fish.

Grill the galangal rings to aromatise. Remove from the heat and cool. Grill (or char grill) the duck meat to medium or to your taste, remove and cut into thin slices.

Mix the duck slices with the galangal slices and chop together coarsely to create a chunky mixture. Set aside.

Simmer the offal in the stock for 20 minutes, remove, strain, cool and slice thinly.

In a bowl mix the fish sauce, lime juice and sugar until dissolved then add the dried chilli. Now add the duck mixture, the offal slices, shallots, mint leaves, onion, spring onion, coriander and roasted rice.

Mix thoroughly, garnish with chillies and serve with salad ingredients and sticky rice.

Serves: 4   Prep time: 40 mins   Cooking time: 25 mins

larb gai
chicken salad with chilli, lime & mint

250g chicken fillets

2 tbsp chicken stock

2 tbsp fish sauce

2 tbsp lime juice

½ tsp toasted ground dried chilli

1 tsp sugar

1 tbsp toasted ground rice
(see page 242)

handful mint leaves

handful coriander,
chopped

1 tbsp finely sliced shallots

1 spring onion,
chopped

1 tsp finely chopped galangal

2 hot chillies,
finely chopped

To serve:

lettuce leaves

sliced cucumber

mint leaves

raw snake beans

coriander leaves

Thai eggplant

spring onion

fresh chilli

sticky rice
(see page 242)

Mince the chicken fillet, but not too finely.

Bring the stock to the boil in a pan, then add the minced chicken and stir while the chicken cooks (about 5 minutes). Remove from the heat.

In a bowl combine the fish sauce, lime juice, dried chilli, fresh chilli and sugar. Mix well then add the cooked chicken. Stir to mix, then add the toasted rice, mint leaves, coriander, shallots, spring onions, lemongrass and galangal and mix together.

Serve garnished with mint and coriander leaves, spring onion, sfresh chilli rings, fresh lettuce, cucumber, Thai eggplant and snake beans to complement the larb.

Serves: 4   Prep time: 20 mins   Cooking time: 15 mins

nuer nam tok

waterfall beef salad

500g Scotch fillet or sirloin steak

2 tbsp fish sauce

2½ tbsp lime juice

1 tsp sugar

3 shallots,
peeled and finely chopped

handful coriander leaves,
finely chopped

handful mint leaves

2 tbsp ground toasted rice
(see page 242)

2 tsp ground toasted dried chilli
(see page 242)

to serve:

spring onions

lettuce

cucumber

This dish is well named as, when you grill the steak, the juices run out like a waterfall onto the charcoal, sizzling and smoking, which means it is done. Traditionally this is served rare.

Grill the steak until the juice begins to run out, then remove from the heat and slice into thin, bite-sized pieces and set aside.

In a bowl combine the fish sauce, lime juice and sugar and mix until the sugar dissolves. Add the beef and the rest of the ingredients, mix well, garnish, then serve with salad ingredients such as lettuce, cucumber and spring onions.

Serves: 4   Prep time: 20 mins   Cooking time: 15 mins

goong chae num pla
prawns with fiery chilli fish sauce

200g uncooked medium-sized prawns

2 tbsp lime juice

1½ tbsp fish sauce

1 tsp sugar

12 chillies,
finely chopped

6 cloves garlic,
peeled and finely chopped

handful coriander leaves

1 tbsp salmon roe

finely sliced garlic,
to garnish

mint leaves,
to garnish

chilli rings,
to garnish

Remove the prawn heads and the shells, keeping the tail on then de-vein. Transfer the prawns to a plate, cover and place in the fridge to chill.

In a bowl place lime juice, fish sauce and sugar, mix well, then add the chilli, garlic and coriander to make the sauce.

Remove the prawns from the fridge just before serving and arrange on a plate, topped with the chilli fish sauce, salmon roe, slices of garlic, mint leaves and chilli rings.

Serves: 4   Prep time: 20 mins

sai gork isan
isan sour & spicy sausage

500g pork

2 stems lemongrass,
sliced

1 knob galangal,
sliced

3 kaffir lime leaves,
finely chopped

handful coriander leaves,
finely chopped

1 chilli,
finely chopped

5 cloves garlic,
peeled and coarsely chopped

½–¾ tbsp salt,
to taste

½ tbsp finely ground white pepper

150g cooked sticky rice

1-m sausage casing,
bought from the butcher

These very tasty sausages from the Isan region are available all over Thailand and differ from the sai ouar, Chiang Mai sausages in that the pork is preserved, Isan-style, for a few days before cooking.

In the bowl combine all the ingredients except the sausage casings and use your hands to mix well.

Stuff the sausage casing, twisting to form individual sausages as you go. Cover and keep in a cool place, but not the fridge, for 2–3 days, until the sausages go sour. Transfer to the fridge to keep until you are ready to cook the sausages.

Prick the sausages a few times with a fork and barbecue or grill until cooked.

Serves: 12   Prep time: 25 mins + 3 days to preserve
Cooking time: About 5–7 mins

khao neaw, gai yang, som tum

sticky rice with bbq chicken & green papaya salad

This classic Isan combination is so addictive that at least a hundred thousand servings must be consumed every day throughout Thailand.

khao neaw – sticky rice

250g sticky rice

1.5 litres cold water

som tum – green papaya salad

2 cloves garlic, peeled

5–10 bird's eye chillies, to taste

1 tbsp roasted peanuts

½ tbsp dried shrimps

2 snake beans cut in x 7.5-cm pieces

8 cherry tomatoes, halved

2 tbsp lime juice, to taste

1½ tbsp fish sauce, to taste

½ tbsp palm sugar, to taste

150g shredded green papaya

Gai yang Isan – Isan BBQ chicken

1x1.5kg free-range chicken

2 cloves garlic

2 coriander roots

2 tsp caster sugar

1½ tbsp light soy sauce

2 tsp ground pepper

½ tsp salt

Sticky rice: Rinse the sticky rice and soak in cold water overnight. Rinse again then place it in a bamboo basket steamer to steam over boiling water for 15–20 minutes. If you don't have a bamboo steamer, place the sticky rice on top of a clean cloth on the bottom of a stainless steel steamer.

As soon as the rice is cooked, ladle it out with a wooden spoon onto a flat surface or tray to release the steam and remove the moisture. This is the traditional Isan method to ensure that when the rice cools it will not stick to your hands.

Green papaya salad: Using a large pestle and mortar (traditionally clay), pound the garlic, chilli, peanuts and dried shrimps to a rough paste. Add the green beans and tomatoes and pound a few times to bruise the beans and release the juice from the tomatoes.

Season with lime juice, fish sauce, sugar, add the papaya and mix well taking care not to break up the shreds.

Isan BBQ chicken: Cut the chicken in half lengthways using poultry shears. To make the marinade, pound the garlic and coriander using a pestle and mortar, then transfer to a larger bowl and add the sugar, soy sauce, pepper and salt.

Put the chicken halves on a plate and rub the marinade mixture all over them. Cover with cling film and leave in the fridge overnight or at least for 3–4 hours.

When you are ready, barbecue or grill the chicken for 15–20 minutes over medium heat, then slice to serve.

Serve with the sticky rice and hot barbecued chicken with extra chilli, fish sauce and/or lime juice to add to taste.

Serves: 4   Prep time: 1 hour   Cooking time: 1 hour

soup nor mai
bamboo shoot salad with chilli & sesame

250g bamboo shoots,
finely shredded

120ml water

2–4 hot chillies,
finely sliced

2 garlic cloves, peeled

2 shallots,
peeled and finely chopped

2 tbsp fish sauce

2 tbsp lime juice

1 tbsp ground toasted rice
(see page 242)

1 tsp toasted sesame seeds

handful mint leaves

handful coriander leaves,
chopped

1 spring onion,
finely chopped

Bamboo grows profusely everywhere in Thailand and the young shoots are used as a vegetable. This dish comes from the Northeast and, while it is called a soup in Isan Thai, it is actually a spicy salad that goes perfectly with sticky rice.

Boil the shredded bamboo shoots in a pan of water for 5 minutes until tender. Remove and drain.

Heat a frying pan over a medium heat and dry-fry the chilli, garlic and shallots for 5 minutes or until brown, being careful not to burn them. Transfer to a mortar and pound with the pestle to a rough paste.

Place the paste in a bowl with the fish sauce and lime juice. Add the bamboo shoots and toasted rice and mix well.

Serve garnished with sesame seeds, mint leaves, coriander and chopped spring onion.

Serves: 4   Prep time: 25 mins   Cooking time: 15 mins

naem sod
sour & spicy pork in banana leaves

500g minced pork

1½ tsp sea salt

120g cooked pork skin,
finely sliced

5 garlic cloves,
peeled and finely sliced

8 small whole hot chillies

8 banana leaves,
30-cm x 30-cm

juice of 2 limes

1 knob ginger,
finely sliced

1 shallot,
finely sliced

handful coriander leaves

handful mint leaves

1 tbsp roasted peanuts

large crisp lettuce leaves

whole hot chillies,
to taste

In Isan, naem sod is an everyday snack to go with drinks. The minced pork is made by fermenting pork and pork skin with salt, garlic and chilli, then wrapping it in banana leaves and storing in the fridge for 5–7 days (yes, days!) until the pork goes sour, or traditionally, 3–4 days at room temperature.

It can be served with rice for a sour pork salad, as an addition to fried rice or simply unwrapped and served with a squeeze of fresh lime and a deliciously cold beer.

In a bowl, mix the minced pork with the salt, add the pork skin, garlic and chillies, mix well and balance with extra salt and garlic to taste.

Divide into 4 and roll each in 2 banana leaves to make parcels, secure the ends with ties and store in the fridge for 5–7 days to ferment.

When you are ready to eat, open the wrapper and squeeze the lime juice over the pork. Arrange the remaining ingredients in the centre of the lettuce leaves and serve with the pork, accompanied by hot chillies to taste.

Serves: 4   Prep time: 20 mins + 5–7 days fermenting time

naem khao tod
spicy crispy rice with sour pork salad

350g steamed jasmine rice

2 tsp salt

1 tbsp Red Curry Paste
(see page 238)

4 kaffir lime leaves,
finely chopped

1 litre cooking oil

15 hot dried chillies

2 tbsp lime juice

2 tbsp fish sauce

1tsp sugar

1 Naem Sod
(sour pork, see page 54)

1 shallot,
peeled and finely sliced

1 spring onion, finely sliced

spring onion

handful of mint leaves

1 tbsp roasted peanuts

½ tsp ground toasted dried chilli

handful coriander leaves

to serve:

lettuce leaves

mint leaves

spring onion

cucumber

betel leaves

This traditional Isan snack of crispy rice, sour pork and spicy sauce is balanced by the fresh mint, lettuce and herbs. It is a favourite for a light lunch, but please note that one of the ingredients is fermented sour pork which takes 5–7 days to make.

Place the rice in a bowl, add salt, red chilli paste and kaffir lime leaves, mix evenly then roll into the size of golf balls.

Heat the oil in a deep pan, add the rice balls to deep-fry until golden brown, remove and drain on paper towels. In the same pan, fry the dried chilli until crisp, then remove and drain on paper towels and break into bite-sized pieces.

In a bowl combine the lime juice, fish sauce and sugar and mix until the sugar dissolves. Open the parcel of sour pork, break it into bite-sized pieces. Place in a bowl and add crispy rice, shallot, spring onions, mint leaves, nuts, dried chilli powder and coriander.

Mix well then serve on a plate topped with dried chillies and a few mint leaves. Surround with lettuce leaves, mint leaves, spring onion, cucumber and betel leaves.

Serves: 4   Prep time: 45 mins + 5–7 days fermenting time
Cooking time: 15 mins

The Mighty Mekong

The 'mother of all rivers' forms the border with Laos around Isan in Northeastern Thailand. One of the world's great rivers, the legendary Mekong provides a valuable source of food and a means of travel between the river ports.

Elaborate stone temples are the signature of the Khmer empire, featuring distinctively tiered towers and intricate carving.

water serpents

Revered throughout Asia, mythical serpents (naga) are an integral part of temple architecture and the Mekong River is regarded as one of their spiritual homes.

cliff paintings

The 1500BC cliff paintings at Pha Taem on the banks of the Mekong near Khong Chiam feature geometrical designs, huge figures, hand prints, fish traps, animals and fish.

rain-making festivals

The Mekong River floods and cuts the area off for some months of the year. Deforestation has left plains which are irrigated but rainfall is unpredictable and the subject of many rain-making festivals.

Khmer influence

Southern Isan is particularly known for its strong Khmer influence with many beautiful temples and ruins to see. The Khorat Plateau came under the rule of Cambodia from the ninth to the fourteenth centuries and most of the imposing temples were built during this time.

stone temples

On the ancient route between Angkor and the Khorat Plateau, Prasat Hin Khao Phnom Rung and Prasat Hin Phima are restored examples of Khmer architecture.

Influences

Isan food

The food of Isan is very simple with fish from the rivers and sticky (glutinous) rice served with practically everything. Although sticky rice is an Isan staple, the Khorat plateau is a major producer of Jasmine rice.

grilling

Until the 16th century when the Chinese brought the wok, meats and fish were grilled and this is still a traditional way of cooking in Isan.

giant mekong catfish

The Mekong is a wonderful source of fish. When the river is low during April and May the giant catfish are caught. This expensive delicacy is enjoyed at the best restaurants in the season.

Ubon Ratchathani

Famous for its duck salad, the city was founded by Lao immigrants although Ubon province was first part of the Khmer Empire from the 10th century and later ruled by Ayutthaya.

"People always ask me about my birthplace and when I tell them that I was born on the Mekong River they are always fascinated as it such a legend, evoking a sense of adventure and excitement. Literally translated, sai mae nam means flow of the mother river and, for those who grow up along its banks, the 'Mae Kong' is a part of us, the nurturing source of life.

Warmed by golden sun, washed by monsoon
rains and fed by meandering rivers,
Thailand's fields are ideal for growing rice.

hor mok pla isan
isan steamed river fish

20g sticky rice

2 tbsp water

1 tbsp Isan Pla Ra

2 stems lemongrass,
finely sliced

2 shallots,
peeled and finely sliced

5–10 hot red chillies,
sliced (reserve some for garnish)

2 tsp finely sliced galangal

1 tbsp fish sauce

2 tbsp lime juice

2 kaffir lime leaves,
finely sliced

2 banana leaves
(30-cm x 30-cm)

300g fish fillets such as barramundi,
snapper or cod

handful sweet basil leaves
(reserve a few for serving)

handful of Chinese cabbage
or morning glory leaves

Mekong river fish combined with a very spicy paste then steamed in banana leaves is a traditional Isan dish. It brings back some wonderful memories of my youth, hanging around the Mekong River banks with friends and eating fish cooked this way.

Returning to the Mekong recently I found the pace of life much the same and watched the sun set over the river with my friends Ken and Peter. We agreed that hor mok pla with sticky rice and a cold beer is hard to beat.

Pound the sticky rice to a fine paste using a pestle and mortar. Place the rice in a pan with 1 tbsp of warm water in a pan and stir until mixed thoroughly.

In a separate pan, boil another 1 tbsp of water, add the anchovy sauce, stir well, and remove from heat. Pound the lemongrass, shallots, chilli and galangal to a fine paste in the pestle and mortar.

In a bowl combine the fish sauce and lime juice, add the anchovy sauce and rice paste, mix well and add the sliced kaffir lime leaves.

Warm the banana leaves under the grill until they just begin to change colour then remove. On each one place Chinese cabbage (or morning glory) leaves, then fish fillets and top with the paste and sweet basil. Wrap up the parcels and secure with toothpicks.

Cook in a steamer over boiling water for 20–25 minutes until cooked. To serve, open the banana leaves and garnish the fish with sliced chillies and basil leaves.

Serves: 4   Prep time: 20 mins   Cooking time: 25 mins

yam pla dook fu

crispy catfish with green mango salad

300g catfish
or other white fish fillets

sea salt flakes

1 litre vegetable oil

1½ tbsp palm sugar

2 tbsp fish sauce

1–1½ tbsp lime juice

1 green mango,
peeled and shredded

4 bird's eye chillies,
finely chopped

80g toasted cashew nuts

2 shallots,
peeled and thinly sliced

½ tbsp dried shrimp,
finely blended

I grew up with this dish, which was especially enjoyed by my grandmother, my aunties and their friends at the lunch or dinner table. The hot Thai summer is the season for green mangoes and it was my mission to procure them for these hungry ladies. Things were complicated by the fact that there are different types of green mango and I would be in big trouble if I came home with the wrong ones. Crisp, sour green mangoes are the required variety.

Traditional method:

Steam the fish over boiling water for about 10 minutes then dry on a paper towel. Flake the fish fillets with a fork, remove any bones, pat dry with paper towel and sprinkle with a little sea salt before pan-frying in hot oil. Ideally the fish should be fluffy edged and crisp. Remove, drain and place on a serving plate.

In a bowl combine the sugar, fish sauce and lime juice and mix well until the sugar dissolves. Add the green mango, chilli, cashew nuts, shallots and dried shrimp. Mix well and serve with the fish.

Arun Thai Restaurant method:

Many of my customers prefer whole fish fillets. To serve this way, sprinkle the fillets with a little sea salt, heat the oil in a frying pan over a medium heat and deep-fry the fillets until golden brown. Remove and drain on paper towel, then serve alongside the green mango salad.

Serves: 4   Prep time: 35 mins   Cooking time: 30 mins

tom som pla isan
spicy sour fish soup with lemongrass & lime

10 thick slices galangal

5–8 chillies,
to taste

4 shallots,
peeled and sliced

1 stem lemongrass,
finely sliced

800ml fish stock

8 kaffir lime leaves, torn

1 tsp sea salt

500g white fish fillets
cut in to 4-cm x 4-cm pieces

10 cherry tomatoes, halved

2 tbsp tamarind juice

3 tbsp fish sauce

2 tbsp lime juice

120g straw or oyster mushrooms

4 spring onions, trimmed and cut into
4-cm x 4-cm lengths

handful lemon basil leaves

handful coriander,
finely chopped

2 stems dill

This Isan sour fish soup is very clean with spicy flavours and it is very different from the Central and the Southern fish curries. You can also make variations of this soup using chicken (see opposite page) or prawns.

Pound the galangal, chillies, shallots and lemongrass to a coarse paste using a pestle and mortar.

Heat 400ml of the fish stock in a deep pan then add the paste, kaffir lime leaves and salt. Bring to the boil then the reduce heat and simmer for 10 minutes to aromatise.

Add the remaining fish stock, bring back to the boil then add the fish fillets. Lower the heat and cook gently for about 7–8 minutes, until the fish is done. (Don't stir while the fish is cooking as this would break it up, make the soup cloudy and give it an overly strong smell.)

Add the cherry tomatoes and season with the tamarind juice, fish sauce and lime juice, then drop in the mushrooms and spring onion. Continue to cook for about 3 minutes, add the lemon basil and coriander, stir, then serve garnished with dill.

Serves: 4   Prep time: 20 mins   Cooking time: 35 mins

tom som gai baan
spicy free-range chicken soup with tamarind & lime

10 thick slices galangal

10 whole hot red chillies,
to your taste

4 shallots,
peeled and sliced

2 stems lemongrass,
finely sliced

2 litres water

8 kaffir lime leaves, torn

2 tsp salt

1.5kg free-range chicken, chopped
into 3 x 3-cm pieces with the bone

10 cherry tomatoes, halved

2 tbsp tamarind juice

3 tbsp fish sauce

2 tbsp lime juice

120g straw or oyster mushrooms

4 spring onions,
trimmed and cut into 4-cm lengths

handful lemon basil leaves

handful sweet basil leaves,
finely chopped

2 stems dill

Pound the galangal, chillies, shallot and lemongrass
to a coarse paste using a pestle and mortar.

Heat the water in a deep pan then add the paste, kaffir lime leaves
and salt. Bring to the boil then add the chicken, reduce the heat and
simmer until tender, about 30–45 minutes.

Add the cherry tomatoes and season with the tamarind juice, fish
sauce and lime juice, then drop in the mushrooms and spring onions.
Continue to cook for about 3 minutes, then add the lemon basil
leaves and chopped basil, stir, then serve garnished with chopped
basil and dill.

Serves: 4   Prep time: 20 mins   Cooking time: 75 mins

po pia sod isan
isan spring rolls with duck, prawns, chicken & beef

12 rice paper sheets

5 lettuce leaves,
finely sliced

2 cucumbers cut into 8
and de-seeded

80g cooked bean curd,
cut into strips

2 egg omelette,
finely sliced

100g chicken breast,
poached in dark soy sauce

100g roasted duck meat,
sliced into thin strips

100g cooked prawn meat,
sliced into strips

100g cooked beef fillet,
sliced into strips

100g small rice noodles,
cooked

50g finely sliced carrot

80g bean sprouts

handful mint leaves

handful coriander leaves

Tamarind Sauce
(see page 241)

First arrange all the prepared ingredients in separate containers in front of you.

Fill a large bowl with warm water and dip the rice paper sheets in the water, one at a time, to wet them. After dipping, set them aside on a plate – they will be ready to roll in 3 minutes.

Make two of each type, placing the ingredients for each on the spring roll sheets in the order shown.

Duck rolls: lettuce, carrot, coriander leaves, mint leaves, rice noodles, cucumber and duck.

Chicken rolls: lettuce, cucumber, bean curd, bean sprouts, omelette, carrot and chicken.

Prawn rolls: lettuce, cucumber, bean curd, bean sprouts, omelette strips, rice noodles, carrot and prawn.

Beef rolls: lettuce, cucumber, rice noodles, carrot and beef.

How to roll: after the first turn, place one hand on the flat of the sheet while tensioning the roll with the other. Repeat after each turn to ensure the contents are firmly held by the wrapper.

To serve, slice each spring roll in two diagonally, garnish with coriander leaves and serve with spicy tamarind sauce.

Makes: 16   Prep time: 40 mins
Cooking time: 20 mins

nuer dai dait

one sun dried beef

2kg beef rump or buffalo topside

10 cloves garlic

5 coriander roots

2 tbsp coriander seeds

3 stems lemongrass,
finely sliced

3 tbsp sugar

2 tsp salt

1 tbsp ground black pepper

3 tbsp fish sauce

3 tbsp soy sauce

2 tbsp oyster sauce

1 litre oil for deep-frying

Si Racha Chilli Sauce
(see page 241)

In Isan this is a way of preserving meat and having a ready-made dish to enjoy at any time with sticky rice and a cold beer. The name 'one sun' refers to the method of drying the beef in the sun for one day.

Cut the meat into strips, approximately 1-cm x 1-cm x 10-cm.

Pound the garlic, coriander root, coriander seed and lemongrass to a rough paste using a pestle and mortar.

In the bowl combine the sugar, salt, pepper, fish sauce, soy sauce, oyster sauce with the paste and mix until the salt and sugar have dissolved. Add the meat, mix well, then cover and place in the fridge to marinate overnight.

Traditionally, the next day, lay the strips on a big flat tray and place in the full sun until the beef has dried. Repeat if necessary, but one day should be enough.

If your sunshine is elusive, cook in a very, very low oven for 5 hours. Store in an airtight container in the fridge.

When you wish to use, heat the oil in a pan to about 180°C, add the meat and deep fry for 4–5 minutes. The meat can also be char-grilled, if you prefer. Serve with Si Racha chilli sauce.

Serves: 4   Prep time: 30 mins, plus overnight to marinate + 1 day drying time
Cooking time: 5 mins

suer rong hai
crying tiger wagyu beef

500g wagyu sirloin,
or other beef with some fat

marinade:

1 tbsp light soy sauce

1 tsp chilli powder

1 tsp pepper

1 tbsp oyster sauce

1 tsp sugar

sauce:

3 tbsp lime juice

3 tbsp fish sauce

2 tbsp soy sauce

2 shallots,
peeled and finely chopped

handful coriander leaves,
chopped

1 spring onion,
chopped

1 tsp sugar

2 tsp ground toasted dried chilli
(see page 242)

1 tbsp ground toasted rice
(see page 242)

Passed down through the generations, this dish is said to have originated in a village which had a problem with tigers. The big cats would prey on the cattle and the one that made the kill would eat the best meat before the others arrived, making them cry. I believe you may also cry like the tigers when you taste the fiery crying tiger sauce.

Combine the soy sauce, chilli, pepper, soy and oyster sauce and sugar in a dish, add the beef and place in the fridge to marinate for 2 hours.

In a bowl mix all the sauce ingredients together, stirring until the sugar has dissolved.

Barbecue or char grill the beef for 4 minutes each side for medium rare, turning once.

Remove from the heat, slice thinly and serve with fiery sauce.

Serves: 4   Prep time: 2 hours 10 mins
Cooking time: 8–10 mins

moo yang kab
nam jim jiew
bbq pork with coriander & isan chilli sauce

3 cloves garlic, peeled

½ stem lemongrass, finely chopped

3 coriander roots

500g pork neck

2 tsp sugar

1 tbsp light soy sauce

½ tbsp oyster sauce

½ tsp salt, to taste

½ tsp ground white pepper

½ tbsp oil

Nam Jim Jiew (Isan chilli sauce, see page 241)

Pound the garlic, lemongrass and coriander roots to a fine paste using a pestle and mortar.

Cut the pork lengthwise into 4 even slices.

In a bowl combine the sugar, garlic, soy, oyster sauce, salt, pepper and oil. Mix until the sugar has dissolved. Add the garlic paste, mix thoroughly, then add the meat, coat evenly, then place in the fridge to marinate for 3–4 hours.

Barbecue (or grill) the slices and serve with nam jim jiew sauce.

Serves: 4   Prep time: 15 mins   Cooking time: 5 mins

The Spice Traders

Ships have sailed the Straits of Malacca from as early as 600BC. Indians, Chinese, Arabs and, later, Europeans brought precious gifts of spices, chilli and foods from around the globe to Thailand.

Temple styles, mosques and European architecture reflect the history of world influences on Southern Thailand.

Influences

ancient empires

From around the years 600–1200, the Southern peninsula was under the influence of the Srivijaya empire, an ancient Malay kingdom with its centre in Sumatra. In the 13th century the Sukhothai kingdom became dominant followed by Ayutthaya which attracted traders from around the globe.

who brought the chilli?

The colonial influence arrived in the 1500s with the Portuguese, Dutch, Spaniards, French, English and others landing on the West coast, many en route for the Spice Islands. Importantly for all lovers of Thai food today – the chilli arrived courtesy, it is generally believed, of the Portuguese.

resort paradise

Sun, beaches, seafood, hot chilli and spice – Southern Thailand is a resort paradise loved by travellers from around the globe for its beaches, diving and colourful cuisine shaped by its maritime history.

"How can anyone fail to love the exotic tastes of the South? Vibrant turmeric and other spices, shrimp paste, fiery red and hot orange chillies, coconut cream, tamarind, lemon basil, lime, lemon, pungent sauces and fabulous seafood are just some of the ingredients to make your tastebuds tremble in anticipation."

sizzling seafood

Travelling around it is easy to be amazed by the tastes that even simple combinations can provide. Seasoned seafood sizzling on the char grill is the most obvious and two highlights my recent visit were a fabulous dish of grilled sand whiting with fresh turmeric and an equally delicious stir-fried crab with chilli and lemon.

mild and fragrant

As well as the hot, strong flavours found in the South, many Muslim-influenced dishes are mild and fragrant with dry-roasted spices and made with ghee, clarified butter not used elsewhere in Thailand.

fresh turmeric

Used in a wide range of dishes including curries, soups, snacks and desserts, fresh turmeric gives Southern food its vivid yellow colour, although it is actually less strong in taste than the powdered variety. Said to have healing properties it is also used as a dye to colour the robes of the monks.

creamy coconut

Coconuts grow abundantly so coconut cream is used in curries and for stewing vegetables, while palm hearts are used in salads.

sator beans

The long green pods of the sator beans are a familiar sight in the markets and the seeds are loved by Thais who might stir-fry them with prawns, garlic and chilli.

Seafood and spice feature strongly in the lives of the people of the South.

gaeng som cha om goong

sour prawn soup with acacia omelette

2 eggs

salt

pepper

handful of young acacia shoots (cha om)

1 tbsp oil for frying

800ml fish stock

1 tbsp Gaeng Som Paste (see page 235)

1 tbsp lime juice

1 tbsp tamarind juice

1–1½ tbsp fish sauce

½ tbsp palm sugar

12 uncooked prawns, peeled and de-veined

Spicy sour prawn or fish soup is very popular in Thailand and traditionally cooked with the fresh catch-of-the-day. The fish used in Thailand is called pla chon but any white fish or prawns will work well. The taste should be sour, spicy and salty, balancing the richness of the fish stock.

Whip the eggs with a little salt and pepper and fold in the acacia shoots. Heat the oil in a frying pan, add the egg mixture and fry until golden. Remove, slice into 8 wedges and set aside.

Heat the fish stock in a pot, add 1 tbsp of gaeng som paste and stir to aromatise. When just boiling add the omelette wedges and simmer for 3–4 minutes, then add the lime juice, tamarind juice, fish sauce, palm sugar and, lastly, the prawns and cook for 2 minutes.

Serves: 4   Prep time: 30 mins   Cooking time: 20 mins

gaeng pu phuket
phuket curried crab noodles

500ml coconut milk

2 tbsp Seafood Curry Paste
(see page 234)

3 kaffir lime leaves, torn

2 tbsp fish sauce

2 tbsp sugar

5 blue swimmer crabs

handful of betel leaves

1 large red chilli, finely sliced

300g thin rice noodles

The Andaman Sea is a rich source of seafood for Thailand and freshly-caught crab is a speciality used locally in all kinds of dishes.

Boil the crabs in water for 15 minutes, then remove, drain and cool. Remove the meat and keep the claws for garnish.

Heat 100ml of the coconut milk in a pan and stir in the seafood curry paste. Stir well and cook until oil from the paste separates, then add the remainder of the coconut milk. Stir well, then add the kaffir lime leaves, season with fish sauce and sugar and stir for a further 5 minutes.

Add the crab meat, cook for 3–4 minutes then add the betel leaves, stir and add the sliced chilli. While the crab is cooking, boil the noodles in water for 4 minutes until cooked, then drain and place on a serving plate.

Spoon the curried crab onto the noodles and serve with the chilled leaves and vegetables such as shredded carrot, bean sprouts, lettuce and mint leaves to the side as a cooling accompaniment.

Serves: 4   Prep time: 20 mins + Seafood Curry Paste 30 mins
Cooking time: 10 mins

khao yam
southern thai rice salad

500g steamed jasmine rice

2 tbsp toasted shredded coconut

100g pomelo or pink grapefruit

50g dried shrimps,
finely blended

100g snake or green beans,
sliced into rings

2 stems lemongrass, finely sliced

2 hot chillies, finely chopped

2 kaffir lime leaves,
sliced into thin strands

1 shallot, peeled and finely chopped

1 tsp ground toasted dried chilli

1 lime cut into quarters

100g green mango, shredded

Khao Yam Sauce
(see page 240)

There are many styles of Khao Yam in Thailand. This is the original Southern style. Don't be put off by the preserved fish sauce as it is an important ingredient which helps to balance the flavours.

For each serving, press steamed rice into a small bowl then turn out into the middle of a serving plate and encircle with small piles of the other fresh ingredients.

When ready to serve, pour the khao yam sauce and lime over the rice and enjoy by mixing all the ingredients together.

Serves: 4   Prep time: 30 mins
Cooking time: 60 mins including khao yam sauce

yum goong mungrong
grilled lobster salad

1.5kg whole uncooked lobster

2 tbsp fish sauce

2 tbsp lime juice

½ tbsp sugar

1½ tbsp Roasted Chilli Paste
(see page 239)

2 shallots,
peeled and finely chopped

1 tbsp roasted cashew nuts

½ tsp ground toasted dried chilli

½ tsp ground dried shrimp

1½ tbsp coconut milk

1 tbsp crispy fried shallots

1 big red chilli,
finely sliced

2 coriander leaves

Cut the lobster in half using kitchen scissors. Remove the head and tail and set aside.

Heat the grill to 180°C and grill the lobster halves, head and tail. After 7–10 minutes the meat will change colour to pinkish white. Remove the halves from the grill but continue to cook the head and tail for a further 5 minutes. Remove and set aside for garnish.

Scoop the lobster meat from the shell, de-vein and slice into bite-sized medallions.

In a bowl combine the fish sauce, lime juice and sugar and mix until the sugar dissolves. Add the roasted chilli paste and coconut milk, mix well to combine, then add the lobster meat, shallot, cashew nuts, toasted dried chilli powder and ground dried shrimp.

Mix well and serve garnished with fried shallots, crispy fried chillies, sliced chilli and coriander leaves

Serves: 4   Prep time: 25 mins   Cooking time: 15 mins

pu pad pon karee
stir-fried mud crab with yellow curry sauce

4 chillies

4 cloves garlic, peeled

2 mud crabs

2 tbsp chicken stock

250ml fresh milk

2 eggs

2 tbsp soy sauce

1 tbsp fish sauce

2 tbsp oyster sauce

1 tbsp yellow curry powder

2 onions, peeled and finely chopped

2 stems Chinese celery, sliced x 7.5-cm long

5 spring onions, trimmed and sliced x 7.5-cm long

2 large chillies, diagonally sliced

Since we opened the Arun Thai Restaurant we have served this very popular dish of mud crab stir-fried with yellow curry. The recipe is from a family friend who serves it for special occasions and so I would like to share this recipe with all my friends who love mud crabs.

Use a brush to clean the crab under running water. Use a cleaver to chop off the two claws and the back of it to crack them, then chop into two at the joint. Now flip the body on its back and chop in half being careful not to cut through the outer shell.

Hold the crab firmly upside down with one hand and use your other hand's thumb and forefinger to prise the body half away from the shell. Repeat with the other half.

Now remove all the guts and feathery lungs from each half under running water. Chop the tips off the legs. Now chop off the base of the claws and chop between the remaining legs. You now should have three pieces plus the two pieces of the claw from each half. Set aside on a strainer. Repeat with the other crab.

Crush the chilli and garlic. Heat the oil in a wok and stir-fry the chilli and garlic until golden brown, then add the crab and cook, stirring, until the crab changes colour. Now add 2 tablespoons of stock, cover with the wok lid and cook for 5 minutes.

While it is cooking, whisk the milk and eggs in a bowl then pour into the wok. Stir well while adding the soy sauce, fish sauce, oyster sauce and curry powder. Keep stirring then add the onion, Chinese celery, shallots and sliced chillies.

Stir well for 3 minutes until the crab is cooked and combined with the sauce. Remove from the wok.

On a big serving plate reassemble the crab, placing the legs and the claws first.

Pour over the sauce and cap with the outer shell of the crab. Garnish with coriander leaves.

Serves: 4   Prep time: 30 mins   Cooking time: 20 mins

pla tod kamin

whole pan-fried fish with turmeric

8 cloves garlic,
peeled and finely sliced

1 tsp black pepper

2 coriander roots

2 tbsp turmeric powder

1 tsp sugar

2 tsp sea salt

800g–1kg whole flounder
(or snapper, mackerel,
red mullet, sand whiting)

1.5 litres cooking oil

2 shallots,
peeled and finely chopped

coriander leaves,
to garnish

Using a pestle and mortar, pound the garlic, black pepper and coriander roots together to a paste, then mix in the turmeric powder, sugar and salt.

Place the fish on a plate and coat evenly with the paste, inside and out.

Heat the oil in a wok, add the shallot and fry until golden brown, then remove and drain on paper towel.

Now add the fish to the oil in the wok and fry until golden, about 8–10 minutes, or for longer if you prefer a crunchy texture.

Remove the fish from the wok, drain on paper towel and serve topped with fried shallot and coriander leaves.

Serves: 4   Prep time: 20 mins   Cooking time: 8–10 mins

gaeng hoi kum
spicy snail curry with coconut & betel leaves

2kg snails in the shell

150ml coconut cream

1½ tbsp Red Curry Paste
(see page 238)

small knob lesser ginger
(krachai), finely chopped

100ml coconut milk

2 tbsp fish sauce

½ tbsp sugar

handful betel leaves,
finely chopped

Clean the snails then place in a large pan of water, bring to the boil and cook for 5 minutes. Remove and drain, then use a satay skewer to remove the snails from their shells. Rub the black spots off the snails and rinse under running water to remove any sand.

Heat the coconut cream in a heavy pan, add the curry paste and lesser ginger and stir well until the oil separates. Add the rest of the coconut milk, stir well, add the fish sauce and sugar and cook, stirring for 5 minutes. If the curry is too thick, add 1–2 tbsp water.

Now add the betel leaves and snails and cook, stirring, for 10 minutes. Remove from the heat and serve immediately.

Serves: 4   Prep time: 30 mins   Cooking time: 20 mins

khua kling gai tod
1000 chilli chicken

1 x 1.6kg free-range chicken

2 litres oil,
for deep-frying

handful dried chillies

2 tbsp oil

2 tbsp Khua Kling Paste
(see page 236)

handful kaffir lime leaves
(reserve some for garnish)

1 large chilli,
sliced diagonally into 8

2 tbsp chicken stock

1½ tbsp fish sauce

½ tbsp sugar

marinade:

10 cloves garlic

1 tsp white peppercorns

4 coriander roots

½ tbsp coriander seeds

1 stem lemongrass,
cut into 3

1 tsp salt

1 tbsp light soy sauce

½ tbsp sugar

A chilli feast much loved by Southern Thais, this delicious dish can be prepared ahead of time as the chicken is marinated twice in its preparation. The name alone makes it sound fiercely hot but the chicken should be crispy and tasty on the outside and deliciously tender and moist inside.

Pound the marinade ingredients to a rough paste using a pestle and mortar. Add the soy sauce and sugar and mix until the sugar has dissolved. Transfer to a large dish.

'Butterfly' the chicken by cutting through the chicken breast with scissors and opening out. Rub the marinade evenly over the chicken, cover and place in the fridge to marinate for 6 hours, or overnight.

Steam the chicken over boiling water for ½ hour, remove and then return it to the fridge, uncovered, for 3–6 hours until the skin is dry.

Halve the chicken, then quarter. Heat 2 litres of oil to 190°C, drop in the dried chillies and cook for 2 minutes. Scoop out the chillies and drain on paper towel.

Deep-fry the chicken quarters for 4 minutes until the skin is crisp and golden. Heat 2 tbsp oil in the wok, stir in the chilli paste, kaffir lime leaves and chilli, lower the heat and cook, stirring, until the paste separates. Add the stock, fish sauce and sugar, stir and pour over the chicken to serve. Garnish with crispy-fried chilli.

Serves: 4   Prep time: 60 mins + 12 hours marinating
Cooking time: 30 mins

khua kling nuer

stir-fried southern dry beef curry

1½ tbsp cooking oil

1½ tbsp Khua Kling Paste
(see page 236)

4 kaffir lime leaves

250g ground beef

handful pea aubergines

4 snake beans,
cut into x 3-cm lengths

1½ tbsp fish sauce

½ tbsp oyster sauce

1 tsp sugar

1 large chilli,
diagonally sliced

When I was introduced to this classic dry curry from Southern Thailand made by Ell, one of my special Thai chefs, I was blown away by its flavours. This is one of many very hot stir-fry dishes from the South with a paste made with two kinds of chilli, balanced beautifully by the other ingredients.

Heat the oil in a wok, add the khua kling paste and cook until aromatised. Stir in the lime leaves and the beef, cook for 4 minutes then add the aubergines and snake beans.

Cook, stirring, for another 2 minutes. Add the fish sauce, oyster sauce, sugar and chilli and stir for 2–3 minutes until the flavours balance.

Serves: 4   Prep time: 20 mins   Cooking time: 15 mins

gaeng pae
slow-cooked goat with yellow curry

2 tbsp oil

2 tbsp Yellow Curry Paste
(see page 239)

1 baby goat leg, 1kg approx
(ask your butcher to chop it into
3–4-cm chunks including the bone)

1.5 litres coconut milk
(reserve 1 tbsp for serving)

150ml water as needed

2 onions, peeled,
each cut into 6 pieces

5 potatoes, peeled,
each cut into 4 pieces

1 tbsp quality curry powder

3–4 tbsp fish sauce

1 tbsp palm sugar

5 chillies,
finely chopped

1 tbsp fried shallots,
to garnish

coriander leaves,
to garnish

slices of chilli,
to garnish

Heat the oil in a frying pan, add the paste and stir until the oil separates. Add the goat pieces, stir well, then add the coconut milk and bring to the boil. Continue to boil for 5 minutes, then turn down the heat and leave to simmer for 2 hours until the goat is tender but still a little firm. Check from time to time adding a little water if the the sauce seems too thick.

Add the onions, potatoes, curry powder, fish sauce, palm sugar and chilli and cook for 30 minutes by which time the goat meat should be very tender, almost falling off the bone.

Remove from the heat and serve topped with the fried shallots, coriander leaves, slices of chilli and a tablespoon of coconut milk.

Serves: 4   Prep time: 20 mins   Cooking time: Allow 4 hours

Seaports and Trading centres

Due to its central position in Asia, Siam as Thailand was known, became a global cultural crossroads alive with trade routes, strongholds, outposts and thriving seaports. Curved around the Gulf of Thailand, the area is the country's highly productive food bowl.

Stunning temples and Buddhas are found in all corners of the kingdom, some even underground.

historic trading post

One of Thailand's oldest towns on both sides of the Phet River, Phetchaburi is an historic trading and cultural centre where Mon, Khmer and Ayutthayan influences can be seen as it was on the trade routes between Burma (Myanmar) and Ayutthaya.

shop houses

Phetchaburi is an agricultural province and naturally there is a thriving market in the town which has a well-preserved old quarter with wooden shop-houses. The province is famous for spicy fried fishcakes with noodles and desserts including baked custard with mung beans and coconut.

rich farming

Drawn by the rich farming opportunities of the delta, many Mon people from Burma (some of the oldest inhabitants of the whole region) settled here and there is a large Chinese community. Mon curries are a speciality in the Kanchanburi province.

kanchanaburi

Thailand's third largest province is covered with evergreen forests and is the source of the rivers Kwae Yai and Kwae Noi which merge at the city of Kanchanaburi, forming the Mae Klong River. Architecture dates the area to the 4th century but it is now best-known for its World War II – River Kwae history.

Influences

gulf sauces

The Gulf port of Si Racha is famous for its seafood and for the spicy Si Racha dipping sauce made from chillies, garlic, vinegar, sugar and salt to go with local mussels, oysters and seafood. Rayong is a fishing port known especially for its fish sauce.

the best rice noodles

Chantaburi was the last Burmese stronghold in the 18th century. Now surrounded by chilli, rubber and coconut plantations, it produces rice noodles which Thai cooks love to use for the Pad Thai fried rice noodles.

pepper and dried shrimp

The area around Chantaburi produces black and white pepper which is in great demand and dried and processed seafoods such as shrimp, squid, fish paste and fish sauce. The annual fruit festival takes place in May/June and the area is prized for its mangosteens, durians and rambutans.

"Made from anchovies, fish sauce is used all over Thailand in a great number of dishes including meat and chicken. The best is made with fresh anchovies and is naturally fermented, balancing the fish taste and aroma without being too overpowering or too salty."

The Gulf provides the essential ingredients for some of Thailand's favourite sauces.

hoi nan reung sod

oysters with lime & si racha chilli sauce

1 shallot,
peeled and finely chopped

½ tbsp cornflour

3 tbsp oil to deep-fry

2 dozen oysters on the shell

crushed ice

1 tbsp lime juice
+ wedges of lime to serve

1 tbsp Si Racha Chilli Sauce
(see page 241)

finely sliced lime zest,
to garnish

red chillies,
very finely sliced, to garnish

Sydney rock oysters are renowned for their sweet taste. Any small to medium oysters suit the jewel-like appearance of this dish, but larger oysters taste just as wonderful with these Thai condiments.

Mix the shallot with the cornflour before deep-frying in the oil until golden brown. Remove to drain on paper towel.

Arrange the oysters on a bed of crushed ice and drizzle with lime juice. Add a drop of Si Racha sauce to each, sprinkle with the fried shallots and garnish with the sliced lime zest and chilli.

Serve with a bowl of lime wedges.

Serves: 4   Prep time: 20 mins   Cooking time: 5 mins

tom yum goong

king prawn soup with mushroom, lime & lemongrass

3 tbsp fish sauce

3 tbsp lime juice

2 tbsp sugar

1 litre chicken or seafood stock

2 stems lemongrass, finely chopped

10 kaffir lime leaves, torn

1 knob galangal, finely sliced

10 chillies, diagonally sliced

2 tbsp roasted chilli paste

8 large king prawn cutlets

8 button (or oyster) mushrooms

a few coriander leaves for garnish

This is my mother's recipe and one I have used in my restaurant from the very first day. Tom yum goong symbolises Thailand – colourful, pungent, hot and spicy.

In a bowl combine fish sauce, lime juice and sugar, stir well until the sugar dissolves.

Add 1½ tbsp of this sauce to each of four soup bowls.

Heat the stock in a pan with the lemongrass, kaffir lime leaves, galangal, chilli and roasted chilli paste. Mix well and lower the heat to simmer the stock gently for 5–6 minutes.

Turn up the heat to bring the stock back to the boil, add the prawns and cook for 3 minutes. Drop in the mushrooms, then remove from the heat and stir to ensure the flavours are evenly balanced.

Divide the soup between the 4 bowls, sharing the prawns equally. Garnish with coriander leaves to serve.

Serves: 4   Prep time: 20 mins   Cooking time: 15 mins

goong nang phar

angel prawns with coconut

12 raw king prawns

½ tbsp soy sauce

2 tsp sugar

1 tsp cracked pepper

200g tapioca
or tempura flour

120ml cold water

300g shredded dried coconut

1 litre cooking oil

Nam Jim Talay
(seafood dipping sauce,
see page 241)

Clean the prawns, remove the heads and shells leaving the tails on. De-vein by pulling the vein out from the head end. Use a knife to lightly score each prawn 10 times each side being careful not to cut right through them. Squeeze the sides to break the muscles in the prawn flesh. This will ensure they remain straight when cooked.

In a bowl combine the soy sauce, sugar and pepper. Mix well, add the prawns and marinate for 5 minutes.

Place the flour in another bowl, then slowly add 65ml of cold water and mix to a paste to coat the prawns. You will be rolling each one in coconut afterwards so the paste must be sticky, but not wet. Slowly add a little more water if the paste is too thick but be careful not to make it too runny.

Coat one prawn at a time, rolling in the shredded coconut, gently squeezing to ensure the coconut binds well to the prawn.

Heat the oil in a deep pan to around 190 °C and add a few prawns at a time to deep-fry until golden brown. Remove and drain on paper towel before serving with seafood dipping sauce.

Makes: 12   Prep time: 30 mins   Cooking time: 10 mins

gaeng kua hoi mae laeng phu

mussels with gaeng kua paste

100ml coconut cream

200ml coconut milk
(reserve 1 tbsp for garnish)

1½ tbsp Gaeng Kua Paste
(see page 235)

1 tbsp white sugar

100g pineapple pieces

1½–2 tbsp fish sauce

2 kaffir lime leaves,
finely shredded
(keep some for garnish)

1.5kg fresh black mussels,
cleaned

1 large red chilli,
finely sliced

In a pan heat 100ml coconut cream, add the chilli paste
and stir until the oil separates, then add the coconut milk.
and stir well.

Add the sugar, pineapple, fish sauce, kaffir lime leaves
and mussels and cook, stirring constantly, for about 4 minutes until
all the mussels have opened – discard any that do not open.

Now add the chilli, mix and serve garnished with shredded kaffir lime
leaves and coconut milk.

Serves: **4**   *Prep time:* **30 mins**   *Cooking time:* **20 mins**

hoi lai pad prik pao

stir-fried clams with chilli & basil

500g fresh clams in the shell

2 tbsp vegetable oil

1 small red chilli, finely chopped

1 clove garlic, finely chopped

1 tbsp Roasted Chilli Paste (see page 239)

1 tbsp fish sauce

½ tbsp oyster sauce

1 tsp caster sugar

1 tbsp fish stock

handful sweet basil leaves

Rinse the clams thoroughly and drain.

Heat the oil in a wok or frying pan and add the chilli and garlic. Stir-fry until the garlic is golden brown – less than 1 minute. Add the clams and stir them until they open. Discard any that do not open.

Add the roasted chilli paste, fish sauce, oyster sauce and sugar, stir, then pour in the fish stock. Cover and cook for 3 minutes. Add the sweet basil, stir and serve immediately.

Serves: **4**   *Prep time:* **10 mins**   *Cooking time:* **10 mins**

pla muk tod grob
spicy salt & pepper squid

200g fresh squid, cleaned

½ tbsp light soy sauce

pinch of dried chilli powder

1 tsp ground white pepper

1 tsp sugar

200g koki or tempura flour

2 litres cooking oil

1 shallot, peeled and finely chopped

2 garlic cloves, peeled and finely chopped

1 red chilli, finely chopped

handful coriander leaves, finely chopped

½ tsp salt

2 stems coriander, for garnish

Slice the squid tube in half, then slice into diamond shapes and pat dry on paper towels to absorb any moisture.

In a bowl blend the soy sauce, dried chilli, pepper and sugar. Add the squid and mix well. Slowly add the flour, working with your fingers to coat the squid evenly.

Heat the oil in a pan to 190°C and deep-fry the squid until golden brown – about 3 or 4 minutes. Remove and drain on paper towels.

While the squid is cooking, heat 1 tsp of the cooking oil in another pan, add shallots, stirring for 2 minutes (the shallots should be translucent but not brown) before adding the garlic and chilli.

Lower the heat and stir constantly for 1 or 2 minutes until golden brown. Turn off the heat and add the cooked squid, mixing to coat with the garlic/chilli mixture and salt. The key is to keep everything hot so it remains crispy.

Serve garnished with the coriander and chilli rings.

Serves: 4   Prep time: 20 mins   Cooking time: 10 mins

tohu tod grob
spicy salt & pepper bean curd

200g firm tofu

½ tbsp light soy sauce

pinch of dried chilli powder

1 tsp ground white pepper

1 tsp sugar

200g koki
or tempura flour

2 litres cooking oil

1 shallot, peeled and finely chopped

2 garlic cloves,
peeled and finely chopped

1 red chilli, finely chopped

handful coriander leaves,
finely chopped

pinch of salt

2 stems coriander,
for garnish

Slice the tofu into diamond-shaped pieces about 2cm thick.
Pat dry with paper towels to absorb any moisture.

In a bowl blend the soy sauce, dried chilli, pepper and sugar.
Add the tofu and mix well. Slowly add the flour, working with
your fingers to coat the tofu evenly.

Heat the oil in a pan to 190°C and deep-fry the tofu until golden
brown – about 4 minutes. Remove and drain on paper towel.

While the tofu is cooking, heat 1 tsp of the cooking oil in another
pan, add shallot, stirring for 2 minutes (the shallot should be
translucent but not brown) before adding the garlic and chilli.

Lower the heat and stir constantly for about 2 minutes or until
golden brown. Turn off the heat and add the tofu, mixing to coat
with the garlic/chilli mixture and a pinch of salt. The key is to keep
everything hot so it remains crispy.

Serve garnished with the coriander and chilli rings.

Serves: 4   Prep time: 20 mins   Cooking time: 10 mins

pla pad ped
stir-fried snapper with red chilli paste

1kg whole snapper, cleaned

1 litre oil for deep frying

1½ tbsp oil

1 shallot peeled and chopped

1 tbsp Red Curry Paste (see page 238)

4 stems green peppercorns

½ tbsp shredded lesser ginger (krachai)

5 kaffir lime leaves

10 pea aubergines

1 tbsp coconut milk

80g bamboo shoots, sliced

1 tbsp fish sauce

1 tsp sugar

½ tbsp oyster sauce

1 large red chilli, diagonally sliced into 8

handful sweet basil leaves

Pat the cleaned fish dry with paper towel. Lay it down on a chopping board with the fish head to the left and the gut facing away from you.

Use a fillet knife to slice down to the bone across behind the gills, then run the knife along the spine to begin separating the fillet towards the tail, slicing to release the fillet. Repeat on the other side then slice each fillet crossways into four.

Heat the oil for frying and deep-fry the fish head with the bones until golden brown. Transfer to a serving plate, holding the tail up to set in a curve.

Pat dry the 8 fish fillets, then deep-fry until golden brown. Remove, drain and set aside on paper towel.

Heat 1½ tbsp of oil in a pan, add shallots and fry until they begin to turn golden. Add the chilli paste and stir for 2–3 minutes until the oil separates and rises.

Add the peppercorns, krachai, kaffir lime leaves and aubergines and stir-fry until aromatised. Add coconut milk, mix, then add the fish pieces, stirring to coat. Add the bamboo shoots, fish sauce, sugar and oyster sauce and cook, stirring, for 2–3 minutes before adding the chilli. Stir together for 1 minute before adding the sweet basil leaves.

To serve, pour the mix over the fish frame leaving the tail high.

Serves: 4   Prep time: 30 mins   Cooking time: 15 mins

pla raad prik
crispy fish with chilli sauce

800g–1kg whole snapper,
cod, rock cod or bream, cleaned

2 litres cooking oil

coriander leaves,
to garnish

sliced chillies,
to garnish

slices of lime,
to garnish

chilli sauce:

5 cloves garlic,
peeled

5 shallots,
peeled and finely chopped

2 coriander roots,
chopped

10 hot red chillies

1 tbsp cooking oil

3 tbsp tamarind juice

1 tbsp palm sugar

1–1½ tbsp fish sauce,
to taste

½ tsp sea salt

handful coriander leaves,
chopped

To make the chilli sauce, pound the garlic, shallots, coriander and chillies to a fine paste using a pestle and mortar.

Heat the oil in the pan, add the paste and cook through to aromatise. Reduce the heat to low, add the remaining sauce ingredients and stir well until the sweet, sour and spicy tastes are balanced. Remove the sauce from the heat and keep it warm.

Rinse the fish and pat dry with paper towel. Using a sharp knife, cut the fillet away almost to the backbone, starting at the head and working down to the tail. Leave the head on.

Flip the fish and repeat on other side. Use scissors to trim the upper exposed bones from the spine. Use a trimmed satay skewer to force the gills apart, so that the fish can sit on its belly with the fillets butterflied out to each side.

Heat the oil in a deep pan. Lower the whole fish into the oil for 6–8 minutes until crisp. Remove from the pan and transfer to a serving plate.

Serve topped with chilli sauce, coriander leaves, sliced chilli and lime.

Serves: 4   Prep time: 15 mins   Cooking time: 30 mins

chu chee goong mungrong
lobster with chu chee sauce

1kg green (uncooked) lobster

1½ tbsp Chu Chee Paste
(see page 234)

250ml coconut milk

2 kaffir lime leaves rolled & sliced into long
fine strips (keep a few for garnish)

½–1 tbsp palm sugar, to taste

1–1½ tbsp fish sauce, to taste

Chu chee is one of richest of the Thai curry sauces and lobster cooked with chu chee is one of the most popular dishes in my Arun Thai Restaurant. The lobster is complemented by the sweetness of the coconut milk, aromatised with the chu chee paste and kaffir lime leaves and balanced by the fish sauce.

Remove the lobster's head and use scissors to cut down the underside of the lobster tail shell. Slide your fingers between the shell and the meat to remove, then cut the meat in 3-cm x 3-cm medallions.

Place the lobster tail in a steamer over boiling water and steam for 8 minutes, then remove and set aside ready to use for serving.

Heat 100ml of coconut milk in a wok, add the chu chee paste and stir well until the oil begins to separate from the paste. Lower the heat then add the rest of the coconut milk, kaffir lime leaves, palm sugar and fish sauce.

Keep stirring and tasting until the sweet, salty and spicy tastes, the aroma of the curry paste and kaffir lime leaves are balanced. Add the fresh lobster meat and cook for about 5 minutes.

Serve arranged on the lobster tail topped with chu chee sauce and garnished with kaffir lime leaves.

Serves: 4   Prep time: 20 mins   Cooking time: 20 mins

goong satay

satay prawns

12 raw king prawns

2 tbsp fish sauce

½ tbsp finely chopped garlic

½ tsp ground pepper

50ml thick coconut cream

1 tbsp good quality curry powder

1 tsp turmeric powder

2 tbsp white sugar

2 tsp chopped coriander root

12 bamboo skewers

Nam Jim Ajar
(cucumber relish, see page 240)

Nam Jim Satay
(satay sauce, see page 241)

This is the Thai version of satay prawns, a very popular street stall dish. A satay in Thailand is always served with satay sauce and nam jim ajar – cucumber relish. The prawns (or cubes of chicken, pork, lamb or beef) are marinated with turmeric and curry powder. The smell of charcoal grilling is intensified by the aromas of turmeric, curry and garlic, while the rich flavours of the sauce are balanced by the relish.

Shell the prawns leaving the tail on then butterfly them and devein by pulling the vein out from the head end.

Place the prawns in a big bowl and add the fish sauce, garlic, pepper, coconut cream, sugar, curry powder and turmeric and stir to mix well. Cover and place in the fridge to marinate for 2 hours.

Remove from the fridge when you are ready to cook and thread a skewer through each prawn from the tail to the head. Brush with coconut milk and barbecue or grill. Serve with satay sauce and nam jim ajar cucumber relish.

Serves: 4   Prep time: Approx 20 mins + 2 hours to marinate + 5 mins nam jim ajar relish + 25 mins satay sauce
Cooking time: 35 mins including satay sauce

tohu ob

roasted bean curd with soy & mushrooms

3 cloves garlic, peeled

3 chillies

3 coriander roots

1 knob of ginger, peeled

1 tbsp oil

1 tsp white pepper

1 tbsp soy sauce

1 tbsp vegetarian oyster sauce

1 tbsp vegetable stock or water

250g silken bean curd, halved

100g oyster mushrooms

2 spring onions, trimmed

Pound the garlic, chilli, coriander roots and ginger to a rough paste using a pestle and mortar.

Heat the oil in a pan, add the paste and stir to aromatise. Add the bean curd, pepper, soy sauce, vegetarian oyster sauce, stock and bean curd and stir through to prevent sticking. Cover with a lid and cook for 4 minutes.

Open up, add the mushrooms and spring onions, replace the lid and cook for another 2 minutes, then serve.

Serves: 4   Prep time: 15 mins   Cooking time: 10 mins

pet tod grob
fragrant crispy soy duck

4 litres water

2.2kg fresh Peking duck

2 stems lemongrass

5 rings galangal

8 kaffir lime leaves

½ tbsp white peppercorns

5 cloves garlic

5 star anise

2 sticks cinnamon

½ tbsp dark soy sauce

5 coriander roots

½ tbsp coriander seeds

½ tbsp sea salt

1 tbsp rock sugar

4 pandan leaves

2 litres cooking oil

green beans, blanched,
to garnish

slices of red red chilli,
to garnish

duck sauce:

1½ tbsp oil

2 shallots,
peeled and very finely chopped

2 cloves garlic,
peeled and finely chopped

1 hot red chilli,
finely chopped

150ml duck stock

½ tbsp soy sauce

½ tbsp fish sauce

1 coriander root,
finely chopped
½–1 tbsp palm sugar

Boil the water in the large, heavy pan, add the duck, lemongrass, galangal, kaffir lime leaves, peppercorns, garlic, star anise, cinnamon, soy sauce, coriander root, coriander seed, sea salt, rock sugar and pandan leaves, making sure the duck is completely covered with water.

Simmer for 1 hour until the duck is tender, then remove, reserving the stock to make the sauce. (You can keep this 'master stock' in the fridge for future use.) Place the duck, uncovered, in the fridge overnight to dry the skin.

To make the sauce, heat the oil in the heavy pan, add the shallot and fry for 2 minutes, then add the garlic and chilli and stir-fry until golden. Pour in the duck stock, mix well and cook for 2 minutes then add the soy sauce, fish sauce, coriander root and palm sugar, mix and cook for a further five minutes until the sauce thickens. Remove from the heat and keep warm to serve with the duck.

When ready to cook, use a cleaver to quarter the duck. Heat the oil in the pan to 190°C and deep-fry 2 quarters at a time for 4–5 minutes, until the duck is crispy. Remove the pieces and drain on paper towel. Garnish with chilli and beans.

Serves: 4

Prep time: 30 mins + 12 hours drying time in the fridge

Cooking time: 1½ hours

gai tod nam makham piak

crispy free-range chicken with tamarind sauce

1.5kg whole free-range chicken

marinade:

1 tbsp finely chopped garlic

1 stem lemongrass, sliced

3 coriander roots, chopped

2 tsp white pepper

1 tbsp white sugar

1 tsp sea salt

½ tbsp cooking oil

1 tbsp light soy sauce

main recipe ingredients continued, opposite page

Rinse out the chicken and pat dry with paper towel.

Make the marinade by pounding the garlic, lemongrass and coriander roots to a fine paste using a pestle and mortar. Add pepper, sugar, salt, oil and soy sauce, mix well then spread over the chicken, spooning some into the inside as well.

Place the chicken in the fridge to marinate for 3 hours then remove and place in a steamer over boiling water to cook for 30 minutes then cool and return it to the fridge for a further 4 hours, or overnight.

Heat 2 tbsp of oil in a frying pan over a medium heat, add the dried chillies and fry for 3 minutes then remove from the oil. To the same pan add shallots, garlic, coriander roots and fry until golden brown. Remove half, drain on paper towel and set aside to use as garnish.

To the remainder, checking for taste, add the tamarind sauce and palm sugar. Stir well then add fish sauce, salt and water, stir, then remove from the heat, keeping the sauce warm.

1½ litres cooking oil

10 dried hot chillies

2 shallots,
peeled and chopped

2 garlic cloves,
peeled and finely chopped

2 coriander roots, chopped

4 tbsp Tamarind Sauce
(see page 241)

1½ –2 tbsp palm sugar

1½ tbsp fish sauce

1 tsp sea salt

2 tbsp water

handful fine rice noodles

2 coriander leaves,
finely chopped

Heat the rest of the oil in a pot to about 180°C. Quickly fry the fine rice noodles for about 1½ mins until they are puffed up and crispy. Remove and set aside.

Chop the chicken in two and deep-fry half at a time in the same pot of oil for about 5 minutes until the chicken skin is crispy. Remove from the oil, pat dry with a paper towel then chop each half into 5 pieces.

Place a bed of crispy fried noodles on a serving plate, add the chicken, pour over the sauce and sprinkle with the fried chillies and garlic, shallot, and coriander mix.

The secret of this dish is that the chicken needs to be absolutely dry before deep frying and needs to be served immediately after the sauce is added.

Serves: 4–6   Prep time: 60 mins + 7 hours marinating time
Cooking time: 35 mins

gai pad med ma-maung hem maphen

stir-fried chicken with cashews & roasted chilli paste

1½ tbsp cooking oil

1 garlic clove,
peeled and finely chopped

250g chicken fillets,
cut into bite-sized pieces

1 tbsp Roasted Chilli Paste
(see page 239)

1 small onion,
peeled and finely chopped

2 spring onions,
trimmed to 7.5-cm long

100g button or straw mushrooms

1 tbsp fish sauce

2 tsp sugar

1 tbsp soy sauce

1 big red chilli,
finely sliced into 8 pieces

80g cashew nuts, toasted

handful dried chillies

Heat the oil in a wok, add the garlic and stir-fry for
30 seconds until golden brown.

Add the chicken pieces and stir-fry until cooked,
then add the roasted chilli paste. Stir to combine the
paste and the chicken, then add onion, spring onion,
mushrooms, fish sauce, sugar, soy sauce and chilli.

Continue to stir-fry for 3 minutes then serve immediately,
topped with toasted cashew nuts and dried chillies.

Serves: 4   Prep time: 20 mins   Cooking time: 20 mins

gaeng pa jorakei

jungle curry with crocodile

2 tbsp cooking oil

1½ tbsp Red Curry Paste
(see page 238)

1 hot red chilli, finely chopped

50g shredded lesser ginger (krachai)

4 whole stems green peppercorns

10 kaffir lime leaves

300g crocodile meat,
cut into bite-sized pieces

400ml chicken stock

1½–2 tbsp fish sauce,
to taste

100g bamboo shoots

6 Thai eggplants,
quartered

handful pea aubergines

½ tsp sugar

2 tsp oyster sauce

½ tsp white pepper

20g sliced carrot

1 large red chilli,
sliced into 8 strips lengthways

handful holy basil leaves

In the old days, travel through Thailand was a slow process especially when it required a trek through the jungle. People had to utilise whatever was available with meat caught by hunting such as wild bull, venison, rabbit, goat or fish from the rivers such as barramundi, catfish – even crocodile as I have used in this recipe.

Heat the oil in a pan, add the red curry paste and chilli and stir well. Add the lesser ginger, green peppercorns and kaffir lime leaves and cook, stirring constantly, for 3 minutes.

Now add the crocodile pieces and mix through. Add the stock and bring to the boil, cooking for 4 minutes before adding all remaining except the basil leaves.

Cook for 20 minutes, then mix in the holy basil leaves. Serve with jasmine rice.

Serves: **4**   *Prep time:* **20 mins**   *Cooking time:* **30 mins**

meang khum
betel leaf wraps

8 tbsp shredded coconut

1 lime

20 betel nut leaves
(or kale leaves)

1 knob root ginger,
cubed

1 shallot,
peeled and sliced

2 tbsp unsalted roasted peanuts

1 tbsp dried shrimp

1 chilli, sliced

sauce:

½ tbsp oil

2 shallots,
finely chopped

small knob ginger,
finely chopped (½ tbsp)

1 knob galangal,
finely sliced

1 tsp shrimp paste

250ml water

3 tbsp blended dried shrimps

3 tbsp palm sugar

1–2 tsp salt,
to taste

A traditional Thai snack with wonderful flavours that complement each other perfectly. Thais say that if it tastes good it must be good for you and, according to my parents, betel leaves help keep the gums and teeth healthy.

We have served traditional meang khum in our restaurant for 20 years and one of my very best friends, Marion Pascoe has helped us grow the first betel leaves for our restaurant. Thanks to her we now have a betel leaf tree growing in our small garden.

Heat a dry wok to medium, add the shredded coconut and toast to golden brown, stirring all the time. Remove the coconut and set aside to cool.

To make the sauce, heat the oil in the wok, add the shallots, ginger and galangal and stir well to aromatise until the colour begins to change. Add the shrimp paste, stir for 3 minutes then add 2 tbsp water and continue to stir.

Now add the dried shrimp, 2 tbsp of the toasted coconut, palm sugar and salt. Taste and add more salt if necessary. Lower the heat and simmer the sauce for 20 minutes until it thickens and is brown in colour. Remove from the heat and cool.

(The sauce will keep in the fridge for a few weeks in an airtight container.)

Slice the lime into 4 and dice each slice into 8 segments. Serve by arranging the betel leaves and other ingredients including the remaining toasted coconut on a serving plate with the sauce in a bowl. Each guest then takes a leaf or two, adds some of each of the ingredients, spoons sauce on top then folds the leaf into a package ready to eat.

You can also present a ready-to-eat snack by arranging the leaves in a small glass with a selection of the ingredients, topped with sauce.

Makes: 20   Prep time: 60 mins   Cooking time: 60 mins

khao niew dum sung kaya
black sticky rice with egg custard

2 litres water

250g black sticky rice

80g white sticky rice

200ml coconut milk

pinch of sea salt

2–3 tbsp palm sugar,
to taste

2 pandan leaves

sprigs of mint,
to garnish

egg custard:

4 x 70g eggs

200g palm sugar

pinch of sea salt

2 pandan leaves

125ml coconut milk

Soak the black and white sticky rice together overnight in I litre of cold water.

To make the custard, beat the eggs, sugar, salt and coconut milk together in a bowl. Tie the pandan leaves in a knot, add to the egg mixture and stir to release the flavour, then remove the leaves and discard. Place the bowl in a steamer over boiling water and cook for 25 minutes. Remove and set aside.

Drain the rice, then place in a steamer over boiling water to cook for about 15 minutes. As soon as the rice is cooked, ladle it out with a wooden spoon onto a flat surface or tray to release the steam and remove the moisture. This is the traditional Isan method which ensures that the rice will not stick to your hands when it cools.

Heat the 200ml of coconut milk in a pan, stirring as it warms. Lower the heat then add the salt, palm sugar and pandan leaves tied in a knot. Stir until the sugar dissolves and the pandan flavour is infused into the syrupy sauce. Remove the pandan leaves and discard.

Remove from the heat, allow to cool, then slowly add to the sticky rice. Using a wooden spoon, stir until the rice is coated with coconut milk then transfer the rice into 4 moulds such as a small bowls – use different shapes for interesting presentation.

Turn out the rice moulds, top each with egg custard and remaining syrup and serve.

Serves: 4   Prep time: 60 mins + time to soak rice   Cooking time: 45 mins

The Chao Phraya River and the rivers that feed it give their gift of life to the heart of Thailand where mighty kingdoms have always flourished.

Known as the land of gold, Thailand is a country where Buddhist teachings are considered as precious as gold itself.

the chao phraya river basin

Drawn by the fertile flood plains where many rivers meet to form the Chao Phraya Basin, empires struggled for centuries over this highly-prized area.

the mighty powers

From the eighth century, the Khmers extended their empire from Angkor and made their capital at Lop Buri. As their influence declined, the Sukhothai kingdom was founded to the north on the Ping River in the 1200s.

ancient crossroads

Less than 200 years later, Sukothai succumbed to the powerful kingdom of Ayutthaya which became the commercial hub of Asia in the seventeenth century approached by river, sea and overland trade routes.

road to Bangkok

Ayutthaya fell to the Burmese in the mid 1500s but was regained after a duel on elephant back, trading with neighbours and European powers before being destroyed by the Burmese in 1766. Thai rule was re-established at Thon Buri and then across the Chao Phraya River at Bangkok.

rivers and canals

The cities of the plains are linked by rivers and canals which irrigate the rice paddy fields – and were once the main means of transport for people and produce.

Influences

fusion cuisine

Each culture brought elements of its own cuisine and some key ingredients picked up along the way, creating an early global fusion.

smooth and sweet

The food of Central Thailand has a smooth flavour with a touch of sweetness. Green chicken curry made with green chillies and coconut milk has become a familiar Thai taste around the world.

boat noodle soup

A dish from the old days, this hearty soup made from rich stock, meatballs and rice noodles was traditionally served from boats.

yum - thai salad

Salad (yum) is more like tapas in Thailand, food to go with drinks, served as an appetiser or as part of the main course with rice. Yum can be made with seafood or meat with wing beans, fruit such as green mango, chilli, mint, coriander lemongrass, lime and fish sauce to balance the flavours.

"When the early traders brought their precious gifts of spices and chilli they were more valuable than gold, given to the rulers and used in palace cuisine for dishes for the kings."

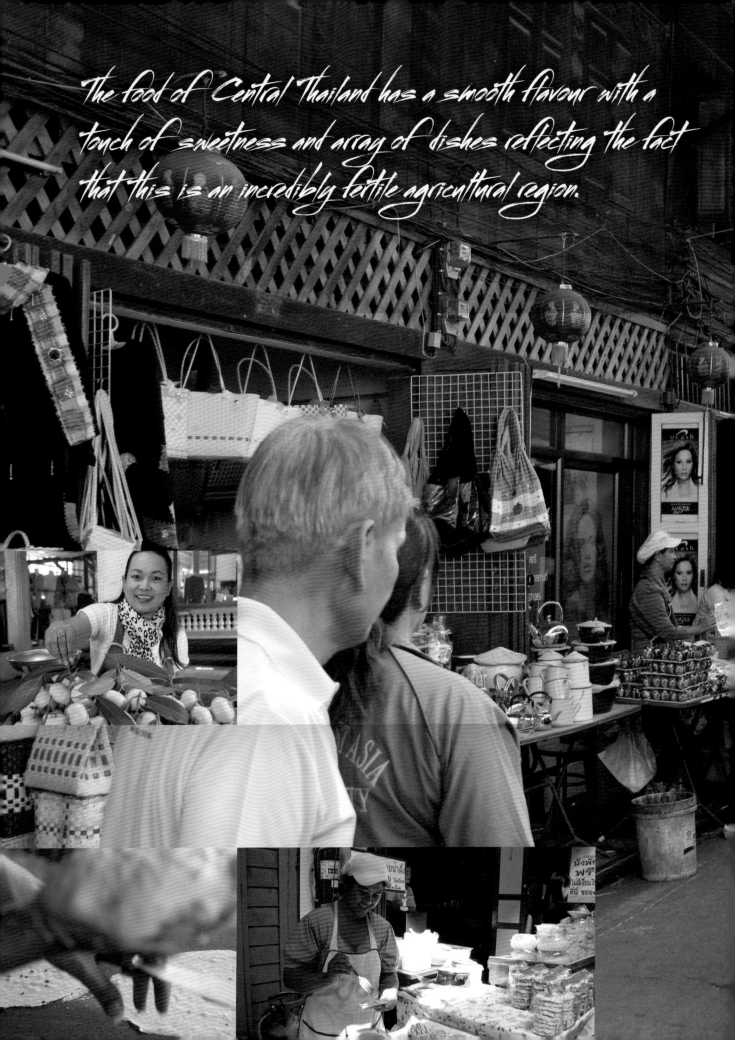

The food of Central Thailand has a smooth flavour with a touch of sweetness and array of dishes reflecting the fact that this is an incredibly fertile agricultural region.

po pia sod

fresh spring rolls with tamarind sauce

150ml water

2 cloves of garlic,
peeled and lightly crushed

½ tsp salt

60g bean curd

60g bean sprouts

100g crabmeat,
(or diced prawn meat)

1 x 15-cm cucumber

3 x 25-cm sq spring roll sheets

3 egg omelette,
thinly sliced

finely sliced chilli,
to garnish

a few coriander leaves,
to garnish

tamarind sauce:

1 tbsp oil

1 clove garlic,
peeled and finely chopped

2 tbsp palm sugar

150ml water

4 tbsp tamarind juice

1 big red chilli,
finely chopped

1–1½ tsp salt

2 tsp cornflour,
dissolved in 2 tbsp water

Boil the water in a pan, then add garlic, salt, bean curd and bean sprouts and cook for 4 minutes. Remove the bean curd and bean sprouts and drain, reserving the liquid to replace in the pan.

Add the crabmeat to the pan, bring to the boil and cook for 3 minutes. Remove the crab, drain and pat dry with paper towel, then set aside.

To make the sauce, heat the oil in a pan, add the garlic and cook, stirring, until golden brown. Add the palm sugar, water, tamarind juice, chilli and salt and stir well. Bring to the boil, slowly add the cornflour mix and stir until the sauce thickens. Remove the sauce from the direct heat, but keep it warm.

Halve the cucumber lengthwise, and then slice each half into three strips. Remove the seeds.

Lay a warm spring roll sheet on a flat surface. (After removing each sheet keep the remainder sealed and warm to prevent them drying out or gaining moisture.)

Add a quarter of the omelette strips (reserve a quarter for garnish) and a third each of the cucumber, crabmeat, bean curd and bean sprouts. Try to keep the drier ingredients to the outside, moist ones in the middle.

Roll firmly and, after the first turn, place one hand on the flat of the sheet while tensioning the roll with the other. Repeat after each turn to ensure the contents are firmly held by the wrapper. Cut in to 4 equal pieces. Repeat with the other two spring roll sheets.

Serve topped with the warm sauce and garnish with the remaining omelette strips, slices of chilli and coriander leaves on the side.

Makes: 12   Prep time: 30 mins   Cooking time: 10 mins

chu chee hoi shell

tasmanian scallops with chu chee curry sauce

12 scallops on the half shell

200ml coconut milk
(reserve ½ tbsp for garnish)

½ tbsp Chu Chee Paste
(see page 234)

1 tbsp fish sauce

½ tbsp sugar

4 kaffir lime leaves, very finely sliced
(reserve a few slices for garnish)

1 big red chilli,
finely sliced lengthways

Wash the scallops and set aside to dry.

Heat the coconut milk, add the chu chee paste
and stir until the coconut and the paste separates.
Lower the heat and add all the other ingredients
except scallops and sliced chilli. Stir well, then set the
sauce aside, keeping it warm.

Place the scallops on their shells in a large steamer over boiling water
and steam for 3 minutes. You may have to do these in batches.
Remove, place on the shells, adding about 1 teaspoon of chu chee
sauce to each shell.

Garnish with kaffir lime and sliced chilli.

Serves: 4   Prep time: 20 mins   Cooking time: 15 mins

pla nueng manao

steamed barramundi with lemongrass, basil & lime chilli sauce

800g barramundi fillet

Chinese cabbage leaves

2 tbsp sliced lemongrass

10 sweet basil leaves

2 coriander leaves, finely chopped

4 whole coriander leaves

sprigs of holy basil

2 slices of lemon or lime

1 red chilli, sliced

sauce:

4 hot red chillies

2 cloves garlic, peeled

2½ tbsp fish sauce

3 tbsp lime juice

½ tsp sugar

Barramundi is an estuarine fish native to the north of Australia. The Aboriginal word barramundi means large scales, which is a perfect description. When we opened the Arun Thai Restaurant in Sydney we were delighted to find this delicious fish which is also found throughout Asia and, steamed, is a light and healthy choice.

Rinse the fish and pat dry with kitchen paper. Line a large steamer with Chinese cabbage leaves and place the lemongrass and sweet basil on top. Now add the barramundi, cover, and steam over boiling water for 15 minutes or until cooked.

While the fish is steaming, make the sauce. Finely slice the chilli and garlic together, transfer them to a bowl and add the fish sauce, lime juice and sugar, mixing well until the sugar has dissolved.

Garnish with the finely chopped and whole coriander leaves, holy basil and slices of lemon or lime and chilli.

Serves: 4   Prep time: 15 mins   Cooking time: 20 mins

pu nim tod bai toei

salt & pepper pandan crab

2 x 150g fresh soft-shelled crabs, cleaned

½ tbsp light soy sauce

pinch of dried chilli powder

1 tsp ground white pepper

1 tsp sugar

200g koki or tempura flour

50–80ml cold water

2 litres oil

2 pandan leaves, cut into x 7.5-cm pieces

1 shallot, peeled and finely chopped

½ tbsp chopped garlic

1 chilli, sliced into rings

pinch of salt

coriander for garnish

Nam Jim Ajar Relish (cucumber relish, see page 240)

Pat the crabs dry with paper towels ensuring no moisture remains.

In a bowl blend the soy sauce, dried chilli, pepper and sugar. Add the crabs and mix well.

In a separate bowl combine the flour and water to make a batter, using your fingers. When it begins to stick to your fingers, add the crabs and coat them evenly with the batter.

In a deep pan, heat enough oil to cover the crabs to 190°C and deep-fry the crabs until golden brown – about 4 minutes. Remove and drain on paper towels.

While the crabs are cooking, heat 2 tsp of the cooking oil in another pan, add the pandan leaves and shallots and cook, stirring, for 3 minutes (the shallots should be translucent but not brown) before adding the garlic and chilli. Lower the heat and stir constantly for 2 minutes until golden brown.

Turn the heat off, add the cooked crabs, mixing to coat with the garlic/chilli mixture and a pinch of salt. The key is to keep everything hot so it remains crispy. Serve garnished with the coriander and chilli rings with a side dish of nam jim ajar (cucumber relish).

Serves: 4   Prep time: 20 mins   Cooking time: 10 mins

kuay jub
slow-cooked pork belly noodle soup

2 litres oil for deep frying

2kg pork belly, skin on

7 litres water

2kg pork leg bones

5 star anise

2 cinnamon sticks

2 tsp whole white peppercorns

5 coriander roots

2 tbsp rock sugar

10 cloves garlic, peeled

2 whole bulbs of pickled garlic
(see page 242)

2 tbsp dark soy sauce

2–3 tbsp light soy sauce

2 tsp salt, to taste

150g firm bean curd

250g mixed pork offal

400g flat noodles,
diamond cut

100g bean sprouts

2 eggs,
hard-boiled and halved

1 tbsp Garlic Oil
(see page 240)

1 tsp ground white pepper

2 spring onions, sliced into rings

handful coriander leaves, finely chopped

2 tbsp Vinegar Chillies
(see page 242)

1 tbsp dried chilli powder

1 lime,
cut into 4

Immigrants from Southern China introduced kuay jub to Thailand more than 100 years ago. The dish is a pork noodle soup with pork offal but don't be put off by this, the flavour is fantastic.

Heat the oil in a deep pan and deep-fry the pork belly for 5 minutes until the skin is crispy.

Remove, drain and slice into 2.5-cm x 7.5-cm pieces.

Boil 5 litres of water in a large pan and add the pork belly, pork bones, star anise, cinnamon, pepper, coriander roots, sugar, garlic, pickled garlic, soy sauces and salt. Boil for 5 mins then turn down the heat to simmer for 1 ½ – 2 hours till the meat is tender, removing the foam from the surface from time to time.

When tender, drop in the bean curd. Cook for 5 minutes, then remove the bean curd, slice into fingers 2-cm x 5-cm and set aside.

Measure 1½ litres of the pork stock and transfer to a separate pan. Add the offal and cook for 30 minutes, removing the foam as it cooks. When cooked, remove the offal, slice thinly and set aside.

Boil 2 litres of water, drop in the noodles and cook for 2 minutes, then add the bean sprouts and boil for 1 minute. Remove immediately and divide between 4 serving bowls.

Place the bean curd fingers, halved eggs and sliced offal around the rim and place a ladle of soup and slices of pork into each bowl. Garnish with garlic oil, a little pepper, spring onion rings, coriander, vinegar chillies and serve with a separate bowl of dried chilli to add to taste.

Serves: 4   Prep time: 1 hour   Cooking time: 2 hours

moo tod katium prik tai

pan-fried pork with garlic & pepper

2 tbsp vegetable oil

5 cloves garlic, peeled and finely chopped

250g pork loin, cubed

1½ tsp fish sauce

1½ tsp light soy sauce

1½ tsp oyster sauce

1 tsp pepper

1 tsp sugar

1 spring onion, finely chopped, to garnish

handful coriander leaves, finely chopped, to garnish

This is an example of home-style cooking for Thai families. The younger children don't like too much spice but, while not spicy-hot, this dish delivers delicious tastes and aromas of the fried and soft garlic with a rich sauce to complement the juicy meat.

Heat 1 tbsp oil in a wok, add 1 tbsp of garlic and fry until golden. Remove from the oil, drain on paper towel and set aside to use as garnish.

Add the second tbsp of oil to the wok, heat and fry the remaining garlic for 2 minutes. Add the pork and cook, stirring, until the meat changes colour – about 4 minutes.

Add the fish sauce, soy sauce, oyster sauce, pepper and sugar, stir well and cook for 3 minutes.

Serve topped with fried garlic, spring onion and coriander.

Serves: 4   Prep time: 20 mins   Cooking time: 15 mins

pad see liew
stir-fried beef with rice noodles

200g flat rice noodles

2½ tbsp oil

2 cloves garlic,
peeled and chopped

150g beef fillet,
cut into bite-sized slices

2 eggs

1 tbsp dark soy sauce

100g Chinese broccoli

½ tbsp fish sauce

1 tbsp light soy sauce

½ tsp ground white pepper

1 tsp sugar

vinegar chillies
sliced, to serve (see page 242)

ground chilli,
to serve

Cut the rice noodles into 2-cm strips and separate them.

Heat the oil in a wok, add the garlic and stir for
30 seconds until golden brown, set aside.

Add the beef fillet pieces and cook for about 3 minutes,
then stir in the cracked eggs, mix well then add the noodles
and dark soy sauce.

Stir until the noodles are evenly coated then add the Chinese broccoli
and cook, stirring for 2–3 minutes.

Add the fish sauce, light soy sauce, pepper and sugar, stir to combine
and serve immediately with vinegar chillies and chilli in little bowls to
add as desired.

Serves: 4   Prep time: 20 mins   Cooking time: 10 mins

guay dtiow reua
boat noodle soup with beef

100g beef meatballs, halved

3 litres water

375g rice noodles soaked in warm water

100g Chinese broccoli leaves, chopped in to 7-cm x 5-cm pieces

100g fresh bean sprouts

handful coriander leaves, finely chopped

2 spring onions, finely chopped

½ tbsp pickled vegetables (tan chai)

250g pork crackling

½ tsp ground white pepper

2 tbsp chilli vinegar

2 tbsp Garlic Oil
(see page 240)

2 tbsp dried chilli powder

beef noodle soup:

6 litres water

2kg beef bones

2kg beef shin, cut into 5-cm x 5-cm chunks

6 star anise

10 garlic cloves, peeled

5 coriander roots

2 pandan leaves

6 rings galangal

½ tbsp white pepper

2 tbsp dark soy sauce

1½ tbsp rock sugar

2 tsp sea salt

4–5 tbsp fish sauce, to taste

3 whole pickled garlic bulbs

120g blood jelly

Boat noodles are a legacy from old Bangkok and Ayutthaya. The soup is usually made with beef and has a very rich stock due to the traditional addition of blood jelly to the stock before serving.

Make the soup first. Boil the water in a large, heavy pot, add the beef bones and boil for 30 minutes, then add the beef chunks and the rest of the soup ingredients except the blood jelly and simmer for at least 2–3 hours to make a rich stock. Taste after two hours for balance, removing the foam from the surface from time to time.

Add the meatballs and cook for a further 30 minutes. The flavour should be salty from the fish sauce, rich and sweet from the herbs. Before serving, spoon a little of the stock into the blood jelly, mix to blend then add back into the stock.

In another pan, boil 3 litres of water, add the noodles and cook for 3 minutes. Remove the noodles, drain and divide between 4 bowls, reserving the water in the pan. Add the Chinese broccoli and cook for 2 minutes, remove and drain and add to the bowls with the uncooked bean sprouts.

Now add the soup and beef and garnish with coriander, spring onion, pickled vegetable and pork crackling and serve with pepper, chilli vinegar, garlic oil and chilli powder in separate little dishes to add as required.

*Serves: 4   Prep time: **30 mins**   Cooking time: **3 hours***

yum thua phu
wing bean salad

120g wing beans

500ml water

8 uncooked prawns, shelled and deveined

60g chicken breast fillet, thinly sliced

1 tbsp lime juice

1 tbsp fish sauce

¼ tsp ground chilli powder

2 tsp caster sugar

1 tbsp Roasted Chilli Paste (see page 239)

½ tbsp dried shrimps, finely blended

1 tbsp coconut cream

1 shallot, peeled and finely chopped

1 tbsp cashew nuts, crushed

2 tbsp crispy fried shallots, to garnish

1 stem of coriander leaves, to garnish

4–6 hot chillies, crispy fried to garnish

Tropical wing beans are a vegetable Thais love to eat with spicy dipping sauce. With their distinctive winged star shape, these slightly sweet and somewhat oily beans are available during the winter season in Australia.

Top and tail the wing beans then finely slice across them to produce star shapes. Bring the water to the boil in a pan, add the wing beans and blanch for 30 seconds. Remove the beans immediately.

In the same water cook the prawns for 3 minutes and remove, then poach the chicken breast for 5 minutes or until cooked.

In a bowl combine the lime juice, fish sauce, chilli powder and sugar, mixing until the sugar has dissolved. Add the roasted chilli paste and dried shrimps, mix well, then stir in the coconut cream.

Now add the chicken, prawns, wing beans, shallots and crushed cashew nuts and mix gently so as not to break up the pieces.

Serve on a dish sprinkled with fried shallots, coriander leaves and fried chillies.

Serves: 4   Prep time: 35 mins   Cooking time: 20 mins

The eternal jewel city

Today you can find the very best of everything in Bangkok, the colourful capital with the Chao Phraya River at its heart.

The city's lengthy ceremonial name includes accolades such as the city of the angels, the eternal jewel city and the happy city.

Wat Arun and the Grand Palace with the Temple of the Emerald Buddha are among the dazzling sights.

the grand palace

The home of the King and administrative court for more than 150 years until the beginning of the twentieth century, Bangkok's stunning Grand Palace complex is Ayutthayan in style and includes the Temple of the Emerald Buddha.

royal thai cuisine

The culture of 'Palace Food' is based on the rivalry between the palaces of different regions to produce the very best dishes, served with great attention to detail. Elaborate fruit and vegetable carving is a great skill and a signature of Royal Thai Cuisine.

life on the khlongs

Bangkok was once a floating city on the khlongs (canals) of the flood plain of the Chao Phraya River. In the mid 1800s most people lived on houses built on rafts which could be moved and moored as necessary. Some houses on stilts were also built along the khlongs.

floating markets

Once all food was traded by boat at floating markets – now there are still some examples accessible from Bangkok such as the early morning Bang Khu Wiang, the Taling Chan weekend market and, further afield, the famous Damoen Sadawak Floating markets and Tha Khan markets beyond.

Influences

markets & flowers

Open markets are a must-see in Thailand. Open 24 hours, Pak Khlong on Maharaj Road is where Thais buy the beautiful fresh flowers and food for their daily Buddhist offerings. The colourful Kao Market in Chinatown sells fresh produce and has been in existence since the late eighteenth century.

street food

Bangkok may be an international, cosmopolitan city but its residents just love their street food five or six times a day. There's food on every street corner and each area has a famous dish – it is no surprise to see a limo pull up at a street stall so the occupants can select freshly cooked food to take home.

ready-to-go

Since preparing the ingredients such as curry pastes for Thai food can take time, it's no surprise that busy Bangkok residents use ready-made pastes and buy the fresh ingredients for the dishes they love all bagged up and ready to cook in the wok.

"Wat Arun, The Temple of Dawn, is the inspiration for my Arun Thai Restaurant and a famous landmark on the banks of the Chao Phraya River. Named after Aruna the Indian god of dawn. The prangs (towers) are Khmer-influenced and encrusted with pieces of porcelain, Chinese-style."

Fast, fun, sophisticated, Bangkok is an exciting city of contrasts, loved for its food, shopping and exuberant lifestyle.

gaeng chuet wunsen

get well soon soup

80g vermicelli

50g dried black wood fungus

2 litres chicken or seafood stock

80g Chinese cabbage, sliced

2 coriander roots, chopped

2 garlic cloves, peeled

½ tsp sugar

1 tbsp fish sauce

1 tbsp soy sauce

2 tsp fried garlic

2 tsp white pepper

handful coriander leaves, chopped

1 tbsp Garlic Oil (see page 240)

marinade:

100g minced prawn meat

100g pork or chicken mince

1 shallot, peeled and chopped

½ tbsp fish sauce

½ tbsp soy sauce

1 tbsp garlic

1 tsp white pepper

handful coriander leaves, finely chopped

2 dried black wood fungus, finely chopped

1 tsp rice flour or cornflour

½ tsp sugar

This soup takes its name from one of my regular customers who arrived at the restaurant tired from travelling and with a cold. We cooked him our 'get well soon soup' from my grandmother's recipe. As youngsters she cooked it for us whenever we were ill in bed, bringing it to us with a little rice.

Now the soup is well-known and three customers, Don, Tony and Kathy, who visit frequently, refer to it optimistically as 'get well immediately' soup.

Make the marinade first by combining all the ingredients in a bowl and mixing with your hands. Scoop up the meat then throw it back into the bowl about ten times to tenderise, bind the meat and release air from the mixture. Hand-roll into small meatballs.

Soak the vermicelli and wood fungus separately in warm water for 20 minutes, then remove and drain.

Pour the stock into a pot and add the coriander roots and garlic.

Bring to the boil, then add the meatballs and cook for 4–5 minutes. Add the Chinese cabbage and wood fungus, bring back to the boil and cook for a further 3 minutes. Add the vermicelli, sugar, fish and soy sauce and cook for 1 minute. Stir well and serve immediately topped with fried garlic, pepper and coriander leaves.

Serves: **4**   *Prep time:* **30 mins**   *Cooking time:* **20 mins**

mee grob

crispy noodles with bean curd & prawns

2 litres cooking oil

80g rice vermicelli

100g bean curd (tofu), diced into small cubes

2 eggs

8 king prawns, shelled, de-veined and butterflied

handful bean sprouts

a few coriander leaves, for garnish

sauce:

1 shallot, peeled and finely sliced

1 tbsp oil

2 tbsp tamarind sauce

2 tbsp palm sugar

1 pickled garlic bulb, finely sliced

2 tsp salt or fish sauce, to taste

To make this special dish perfectly, like the prestigious lady cooks of the inner palace courts of King Rama IV and King Rama V, you will require patience and dedication. The recipe has now been passed on to the outer court and, from there, has been taken worldwide by travelling Thai chefs.

Heat the oil in a wok or deep-fryer to 190°C, add the vermicelli and fry until it puffs up. Remove the vermicelli, drain and set aside.

Use the same oil to cook the bean curd for about 2 minutes until brown. Crack the eggs into a bowl and beat them. Reheat the oil then slowly add the beaten eggs to make fluffy omelette pieces ready to top the servings of noodles. Remove and drain on paper towels.

To make the sauce, gently fry the chopped shallots in the oil in a large pan until golden brown, then add the remaining sauce ingredients and cook over a medium heat for about 4–5 minutes. Add the king prawns and cook for another 2 minutes.

Turn off the heat, add the bean curd and noodles and mix well until they are coated with the sauce. Serve garnished with bean sprouts, fluffy egg pieces and coriander.

*Serves: **4**   Prep time: **45 mins**   Cooking time: **25 mins***

pla dib rot det
tuna fish with spicy sauce

250g fresh sashimi grade tuna belly slices
(or kingfish, salmon, snapper
or snakehead fish)

4 garlic cloves,
peeled

6 bird's eye chillies

1½ tbsp fish sauce

2 tbsp lime juice

2 tsp sugar

1 tbsp lime zest

to serve:

handful mint leaves

handful lettuce leaves

cucumber slices

2 garlic cloves,
peeled and thinly sliced

This recipe comes from a fisherman who showed my uncle and I how to enjoy raw fish in the traditional way. Those who live and fish there say that, like a mother, the Mae Nam Kong (Mekong River) never stops giving and offering. The dish has the intense flavours and freshness of garlic, chilli, lime juice, fish sauce and coriander leaves balanced with mint leaves, cucumber and lettuce.

Place the fish on a clean chopping board and use a sharp knife to slice the fish across the grain into very thin slices 0.5-cm thick x 4-cm long. Place fish on a plate and chill in the fridge for 10 minutes.

Pound the garlic and chilli to a fine paste using a pestle and mortar. Transfer the paste to a bowl and add the fish sauce, lime juice and sugar. Stir well until the sugar has dissolved, then add the lime zest.

Remove the fish from the fridge, top with the sauce and serve with mint, lettuce, cucumber and garlic.

Serves: **4**   *Prep time:* **25 mins**   *Cooking time:* **5 mins**

khao chae

ice rice with condiments

Originating with the Mon people, Khao Chae is just the dish to cool you down in the hot Thai summer. During Songkran, the Thai New Year festival, Khao Chae is a special offering made for friends and guests.

The heart of the dish is fragrant rice made with jasmine flowers and served with tasty dishes of beef, crispy fried shrimp paste, fried sweet pepper, sweet fried fish, fried shallots and steamed vegetables.

King Rama V promoted Thai culinary art and Khao Chae is one of the best examples, certainly one of his favourites which is how it became a dish to serve to kings and queens.

ice rice

10 jasmine flowers

3 litres pure rain water
or non-sparkling mineral water

250g cooked jasmine rice
(use vintage rice)*

1 cup crushed ice

Add the jasmine flowers to the 3 litres of water, cover and leave overnight to infuse. Rinse the rice under cold running water to remove the starch and separate the grains. Set aside to dry for 10–15 minutes then add the rice to the jasmine water. You will need the ice when you are ready to serve.

vintage rice*

Rice (khao) is synonymous with Thailand, and an essential part of everyday living. Like good wine, Thais can even tell the vintage of the rice they are buying – rice matures at different times producing early, middle and late season crops which Thais are proud to be able to distinguish. The rice used in khao chae should be vintage rice which keeps its shaped when it is cooked – you can create your own vintage rice by drying jasmine rice in the sun or in the oven at a very low heat.

hua chai poe – salted radish

1 tbsp oil

100g finely shredded salted radish

1 tbsp palm sugar

Heat the oil in a pan, add the radish
and palm sugar and fry to combine.
Remove from the heat and set aside.

hom jiew – fried shallots

3 tbsp cooking oil

1 tbsp finely chopped shallots

Heat the oil in the wok, add the shallots and fry
until golden brown. Remove and drain on paper towel.

nuer waan – sweet beef

150g beef rump steak

1 tbsp oil

1 shallot, finely chopped

2 cloves garlic,
peeled and finely chopped

1½ tbsp palm sugar

¼ tsp pepper

½ tbsp fish sauce

Heat the grill and grill the beef until cooked.
Remove, cool, then use your fingers to shred finely.

Heat the oil in a wok, add the shallot and garlic and fry until golden
brown, then lower the heat and add the shredded beef and palm
sugar and mix to balance. Add pepper and fish sauce and mix evenly
to coat the beef evenly. Remove from the heat and set aside.

4 banana chillies,
2 red and 2 green

250g minced pork

60g minced prawn meat

1 tbsp soy sauce

1 tsp caster sugar

1 coriander root,
chopped

½ tsp ground white pepper

1 tsp chopped garlic

2 eggs

1 litre cooking oil

Slice the tops off the banana chillies and use a spoon to remove the seeds and membrane. Pound the coriander root and chopped garlic to a fine paste using a mortar and pestle. In a bowl combine the pork and prawn meat, add the paste and white pepper, soy sauce, sugar and coriander, mix well then use to stuff the banana chillies.

Heat the oil in a frying pan. Crack the eggs into a bowl, beat together and dip the banana chillies in to coat them. Transfer to the frying pan to deep-fry until cooked to golden brown.

Remove, drain and set aside.

To make the net to wrap the chillies, heat 1 tsp of oil in the frying pan over a low heat. Dip a finger in the beaten egg and quickly criss-cross the egg across the pan to form a golden net – work quickly as it will cook as you do this. Remove and set aside, then repeat three times and wrap each stuffed chilli in a net.

*luk kapi – tasty deep-fried
shrimp balls*

100g white fish fillet,
grilled

150g shrimp paste,
grilled (see page 242)

30g lesser ginger
(krachai)

2 shallots,
peeled and finely chopped

1 tbsp palm sugar

1 tbsp coconut milk

2 eggs,
beaten

½ litre oil

Pound the fish fillet with the shrimp paste, lesser ginger and shallot using a pestle and mortar. Add the palm sugar, mix well and use your hands to form small round balls.

Dip the balls in egg batter, heat the oil in a deep pan and deep-fry a few balls at a time until golden brown. Remove, drain and set aside.

To serve: Add a handful of ice to the jasmine water and scoop evenly into four bowls and serve with the other accompaniments.

Serves: 4   *Prep time:* At least 2 hours   *Cooking time:* About 1 hour

hor mok pla
steamed salmon curry in banana leaves

100g red fish fillet or other firm fish,
such as mackerel

250g salmon fillets,
cut into bite-sized pieces

1½ tbsp Red Curry Paste
(see page 238)

250ml coconut milk
(reserve 1tbsp to serve)

2 eggs

1 tsp shredded wild ginger

2 kaffir lime leaves,
finely sliced

1–1½ tbsp fish sauce

3 green banana leaves
(approx 30-cm x 30-cm)

Chinese cabbage or morning glory leaves

15 sweet basil leaves

red chilli slices,
to garnish

coriander leaves,
to garnish

Blend the red fish fillet and the red curry paste together in a blender, then place the coconut milk in a pan and add the red fish blend, the egg, wild ginger, kaffir lime, fish sauce and stir well in one direction – stirring this way binds the ingredients together so they remain intact when steamed. Add the salmon pieces and mix well.

To make the banana leaves easy to fold, warm them under the grill until they just begin to change colour, then remove.

Now place the fish mixture on a Chinese cabbage or morning glory leaf centred on a banana leaf. Cover with more paste and sweet basil leaves. Fold up the parcel and secure with toothpicks then place in a steamer to cook for 25 minutes.

To serve, open the banana leaves and garnish the fish with coconut milk, sliced chillies and coriander leaves.

Serves: **4**   *Prep time:* **20 mins**   *Cooking time:* **25 mins**

pad thai goong
stir-fried noodles with king prawns & bean curd

250g rice stick noodles (medium)

2 tbsp cooking oil

½ tbsp finely chopped garlic

12 large raw king prawns, peeled and de-veined

2 tsp dried shrimps

2 duck (or large chicken) eggs

3 tbsp firm bean curd (tofu), cubed

1 tsp pickled radish

1 tbsp chicken stock

1½–2 tbsp sugar

2 tbsp fish sauce

2½ tbsp vinegar

2 tsp paprika

80g bean sprouts

10 Chinese chives

1 lime, halved

2 tbsp finely ground peanuts

2 tbsp chilli powder

2tbsp sugar

World famous Pad Thai is a very popular one-bowl Thai dish. The tasty combination of the sauce, rich noodles, meat and prawns is balanced by nuts, fiery dried chilli and sour lime zest. When I was a boy I would take our own fresh duck eggs to a famous Pad Thai vendor across the road from home to let her cook a special Pad Thai with them.

Soak the noodles in warm water for 30 minutes, remove and drain.

Heat the oil in a wok to medium, add the garlic and cook until it begins to change colour, then add the prawns and dried shrimps and cook for about 2 minutes.

Add the eggs, cook for 1 minute then add the bean curd, pickled radish, noodles and stock and cook for 1 minute. Now add the sugar, fish sauce, vinegar, paprika and half the bean sprouts and stir until the noodles are cooked, then add half the chives.

Serve garnished with the remaining bean sprouts, chives, coriander leaves, lime and peanuts. chilli powder and sugar in a little bowl to add to taste.

Serves: 4   Prep time: 30 mins   Cooking time: 15 mins

hoi shell neung manao

steamed scallops with lime & chilli sauce

60g vermicelli

16 scallops on the half shell

1 tbsp sliced lemongrass

16 sweet basil leaves

handful coriander leaves,
finely chopped

coriander leaves to garnish

sauce:

4 hot chillies,
finely chopped

4 whole garlic cloves,
peeled and finely chopped

2 tsp white sugar

2 tbsp lime juice

2 tbsp fish sauce

Make the sauce first, combining the chilli and garlic in a bowl and then adding the sugar, lime juice and fish sauce, mixing together until the sugar dissolves.

Soak the vermicelli in cold water for 20 minutes then remove and drain.

Wash the scallops still attached to the half shell and place them on a plate which will fit into your steamer. Top each one with lemongrass, vermicelli and a sweet basil leaf each. Now place the plate in a steamer over boiling water and steam for 3 minutes.

(You will need to steam the scallops in separate batches, depending on the size of your steamer.)

Remove the scallops and sprinkle evenly with the lime and chilli sauce then serve on the shell, garnished with coriander leaves.

Makes: **16**   *Prep time:* **20 mins**   *Cooking time:* **5 mins**

sang wa hoi shell
royal scallop salad

16 large scallops

1 tbsp kaffir lime juice

2 tbsp lime juice

2 tbsp fish sauce

1½ tsp white sugar

5–10 hot chillies,
finely chopped, to taste

1 tbsp shallot,
finely chopped

1 stem lemongrass,
finely chopped

1 knob lesser ginger (krachai),
finely julienned

3 kaffir lime leaves,
very finely sliced

handful mint leaves

handful coriander leaves,
finely chopped

1 spring onion,
finely chopped

1 tbsp crispy fried shallots

to serve:
lettuce leaves
cucumber slices

Kaffir lime leaves and lime juice are very aromatic and bitter and used in many classic Royal Thai cuisine recipes. The herbs and spices complement the flavour of the scallops and make this a deliciously tasty dish.

Clean the scallops and pat dry. Heat the grill and cook the scallops for 3 minutes, then turn them and grill the other side for 3 minutes, being careful not to overcook. Remove and set aside.

In a bowl combine kaffir lime juice, lime juice, fish sauce, sugar and chilli and mix well until sugar has dissolved. Now add the scallops, shallot, lemongrass, ginger, kaffir lime leaves, mint leaves, coriander and spring onion.

Mix together, sprinkle with fried shallots and serve with lettuce leaves and cucumber on the side as cooling accompaniments.

Serves: **4**   *Prep time:* **25 mins**   *Cooking time:* **15 mins**

gae pad kapao

stir-fried lamb loin with holy basil

3 cloves garlic,
peeled

5–10 small red chillies,
to taste

2 tbsp cooking oil

handful sweet basil leaves

250g lamb loin fillet,
thinly sliced

handful holy basil leaves

50g chopped onion

2 spring onions,
cut into 7-cm pieces

1 large chilli,
cut in to 8 slices

1 tbsp fish sauce

1 tbsp light soy sauce

1 tbsp oyster sauce

½ tsp white ground pepper

1 tsp sugar

Pound the garlic and chilli together to a rough paste using a pestle and mortar.

Heat the oil in a wok and pan-fry the sweet basil until crisp, then remove and drain on paper towel.

Now add the garlic and chilli paste to the oil in the wok and cook, stirring, for 1 minute. Add the lamb and holy basil leaves and stir for 3–4 minutes until the lamb is cooked to medium.

Add the onion, spring onion and chilli, stir well, then add the fish sauce, soy sauce, oyster sauce, pepper and sugar. Cook for a further 2 minutes, or until the lamb is done to your taste.

Serve garnished with the crispy sweet basil leaves.

Serves: **4**   *Prep time:* **20 mins**   *Cooking time:* **10 mins**

guay dtiow pad kee mao talay

drunken seafood noodles

10–15 hot chillies,
finely chopped

5 cloves garlic,
finely chopped

1 coriander root

1½ tbsp cooking oil

2 shallots,
peeled and thinly sliced

handful lesser ginger (krachai)

5 whole green peppercorn stems

4 kaffir lime leaves

8 mussels on the shell

100g white fish fillet,
cut in to bite-sized pieces

8 king prawns,
shelled and deveined, tails on

8 scallops,
shell off

250g thick rice noodles,
cut into slices x 3-cm wide

½ tbsp black soy sauce

½ tsp ground white pepper

handful Chinese broccoli

handful holy basil leaves

1 big red chilli cut into 8 slices,
lengthwise

½ tbsp oyster sauce

½ tbsp fish sauce

1 tbsp light soy sauce

2 tsp sugar

This is a favourite in Thai bars to have between drinks. Should you have over-indulged, it is the perfect hangover food.

Pound the chillies, garlic and coriander root to a paste using a pestle and mortar.

Heat the wok over a high heat. Add the oil then add the shallots, lesser ginger, peppercorns, kaffir lime leaves and the paste. Stir-fry until aromatised and the paste turns golden.

Add the mussels and stir-fry for about 1 minute, add the fish, prawns and scallops and stir-fry until the seafood has changed colour.

Then add the noodles, black soy sauce, pepper and Chinese broccoli, stir for another 3 minutes then add the basil and red chilli. Mix well then season with the oyster sauce, fish sauce, light soy sauce and sugar. Stir until the seafood and the noodles are evenly combined.

Serves: **4**   *Prep time:* **30 mins**   *Cooking time:* **15 mins**

hoi mae laeng phu ob mor dend

steamed mussels with herbs

1 tbsp oil

1kg mussels in the shell, cleaned

2 stems lemongrass, sliced into strips

5 kaffir lime leaves

3 tbsp fish or chicken stock

½ tbsp fish sauce

50g sweet basil leaves

Nam Jim Talay Sauce (spicy seafood dipping sauce, see page 241)

Steamed mussels were traditionally cooked in a clay pot, but gas cooking in modern Thailand has meant changing to woks or stainless steel pans to cook these aromatic mussels, fresh from the sea.

Heat the oil in a wok, then add the paste and stir until it aromatises. Add the mussels, stir well, then add the lemongrass and kaffir lime leaves.

Add the stock, cover with the lid and steam for 5–6 minutes until the mussels are cooked (the shells open when they are cooked, discard any that remain closed).

Remove the lid, add fish sauce and sweet basil leaves, then serve accompanied by the spicy seafood dipping sauce.

Serves: **4**   *Prep time:* **25 mins**   *Cooking time:* **10 mins**

pad char pu nim
soft-shell crab with chilli & peppercorns

2 x 150g fresh soft-shelled crabs, cleaned

½ tbsp light soy sauce

pinch dried chilli powder

1 tsp ground white pepper

1 tsp sugar

200g koki (or tempura) flour

100–120ml cool water

2 litres + 1½ tbsp oil

1 tbsp Red Curry Paste (see page 238)

1 stem lemongrass, sliced into rings

1 shallot, peeled and chopped

5 chillies, finely sliced, lengthways

2 garlic cloves, peeled and sliced

1 tbsp lesser ginger (krachai)

3 or 4 whole stems green peppercorns

4 kaffir lime leaves

80g sliced bamboo shoots

handful holy basil leaves

1 tbsp fish sauce

½ tbsp soy sauce

½ tbsp oyster sauce

1 tsp sugar

Pat the crabs dry with paper towel ensuring no moisture remains.

In a bowl blend the soy sauce, dried chilli, pepper and sugar. Add the crabs and mix well.

Place the flour into a separate bowl and slowly add the cold water to make the batter which should be sticky enough to coat your fingers. Add the crabs and use your fingers to coat them evenly with the batter.

In a deep pan, heat enough oil to cover the crabs to 190°C and deep-fry the crabs until golden brown and crispy – about 4 minutes. Remove and drain on paper towels.

While the crabs are cooking, heat the oil in a wok, add the chilli paste and stir to aromatise. Add the lemongrass, shallot, chilli, garlic, lesser ginger, peppercorns and lime leaves and stir to aromatise.

Now stir in the the bamboo shoots and holy basil and mix well. Season with fish sauce, oyster sauce and sugar then add the crab and stir gently to combine without breaking up the crab.

Serves: **4**   *Prep time:* **20 mins**   *Cooking time:* **15 mins**

nam prik roung ruae

spicy pork dipping sauce 'bon voyage'

moo waan sweet pork:

3 tbsp oil

500g pork belly,
cut into small cubes

2 tbsp fish sauce

3 tbsp palm sugar

3 shallots,
peeled and finely chopped

nam prik dipping sauce:

10 hot red chillies

15 garlic cloves, peeled

2 tbsp shrimp paste

5 tbsp palm sugar

3 tbsp dried shrimp

1 whole green mango,
shredded

2 tbsp oil

to serve:

2 duck eggs,
hard-boiled, peeled and quartered

crispy fish
(see Yam Pla Dook Fu recipe,
page 68)

crisp lettuce leaves

green beans

Thai eggplant

cucumber

okra

This special dipping sauce dates from the times of King Rama V when it was a favourite dish prepared by the palace chefs to be taken to eat on sea voyages.

Heat 2 tbsp oil in a wok, add the pork and stir until the pork changes colour. Add the fish sauce and palm sugar, lower the heat, add the shallot and continue to stir until the pork is cooked – about 8–15 minutes. Drain and set aside.

Pound the chilli, garlic and dried shrimp to a fine paste using a pestle and mortar, then add the shredded green mango and shrimp and pound to mix.

Heat another 2 tbsp oil in the wok, add the chilli paste and stir until the oil separates, then add the cooked sweet pork and mix to combine. The taste should be sweet, sour, salty and spicy.

Serve with duck eggs, crispy fish, crisp lettuce leaves, raw green beans, raw Thai eggplant, cucumber and okra.

Serves: **4**   *Prep time:* **40 minutes**
Cooking time: **20 mins**

216

gaeng khiao wan gai
green chicken curry

500ml coconut milk,
(reserve 1 tsp to serve)

1½ tbsp Thai Green Curry Paste
(see page 235)

5 kaffir lime leaves

2 tbsp fish sauce

1½ tbsp sugar

250g chicken breast fillets,
sliced into thin strips

3 Thai eggplants,
quartered

50g pea aubergines

handful sweet basil leaves,
(reserve some for garnish)

1 big chilli,
sliced lengthways into 8 strips

Heat 100ml of coconut cream (from the top of the coconut milk) in a pan and then add the green curry paste. Stir to mix well and cook until the oil separates, then add the remainder of the coconut milk. Stir, add the kaffir lime leaves, season with fish sauce and sugar and cook, stirring, for a further 5 minutes.

Now add the chicken, chilli, eggplant and pea aubergines and cook, stirring, for about 4–5 minutes. Add the sweet basil leaves and stir through.

Serve in a bowl, garnished with basil leaves, coconut milk and strips of chilli.

Serves: **4**   *Prep time:* **20 mins**   *Cooking time:* **20 mins**

gaeng panang gai

panang chicken

1 tbsp coconut cream

400g chicken fillet,
thinly sliced

1 tbsp Panang Curry Paste
(see page 237)

400ml coconut milk
(reserve a tablespoon for garnish)

4 kaffir lime leaves,
sliced (reserve some for garnish)

2 tbsp fish sauce

½ tbsp palm sugar

1 large red chilli,
sliced diagonally

Heat the coconut cream in a pan to a medium heat, add the curry paste and cook, stirring, for 3 minutes until the oil separates.

Add the coconut milk, stir well and cook for 10 minutes, then add the kaffir lime leaves and chicken fillet and simmer for about 7 minutes to cook the chicken. Now mix in the fish sauce and palm sugar and continue to simmer for about 3 minutes until the sauce thickens.

Serve garnished with sliced chilli, 1 tbsp of coconut milk and finely sliced kaffir lime leaves.

Serves: **4**   *Prep time:* **20 mins**   *Cooking time:* **25 mins**

gaeng ped pet yang

twice-cooked red duck curry with lychees

1kg roast duck,
(ready-roasted from
Chinese BBQ shops)

500ml coconut milk,
(reserve 1 tbsp of the cream to garnish)

2 tbsp Thai Red Curry Paste
(see page 238)

5 kaffir lime leaves

2–2½ tbsp fish sauce

1 tbsp white sugar

12 whole lychees,
peeled and de-seeded

handful sweet basil leaves
(keep two sprigs for garnish)

2 large red chillies,
sliced diagonally

1 tbsp coconut cream,
to garnish

8 cherry tomatoes

De-bone the duck and slice the meat into 2 x 4-cm pieces.

Heat 100ml of the coconut cream (from top of the coconut milk) in a frying pan, add the red curry paste and stir until paste separates and rises. Stir in the rest of the coconut milk and simmer gently.

Add the kaffir lime leaves and continue to cook over a low heat for 5 minutes, then add the fish sauce and sugar and cook until the oil separates and rises to the surface.

Now add the duck meat, lychees, sweet basil leaves and chilli. Bring to the boil and cook for 2–3 minutes.

Serve garnished with a swirl of coconut cream and sprigs of sweet basil.

Serves: 4   Prep time: 30 mins
Cooking time: 20 mins

yum som o

pink pomelo salad with chilli lime dressing

400g pink pomelo
(or ruby grapefruit)

8 cooked king prawns

½ tbsp chopped chilli rings

2 tbsp fish sauce

½ tbsp sugar

½ tbsp palm sugar

2 tbsp lime juice

120g cooked chicken breast,
shredded

1 tbsp toasted coconut

1 tbsp finely sliced shallots

½ tbsp fried shallots

1 tbsp cashew nuts

2 sprigs coriander leaves

Peel the pomelo, cut off the top and remove the
pithy membrane and seeds. Carefully remove the flesh,
keeping the juicy segments intact.

Remove the shells and tails from the prawns and de-vein.

In a bowl mix together the chilli, fish sauce, sugar,
palm sugar and lime juice to make a dressing.

To serve, arrange the pomelo, prawns, chicken, coconut,
shallots, fried shallots and cashew nuts in a dish or bowl, top
with the chilli lime dressing and garnish with coriander leaves.

Serves: **4–6**   *Prep time:* **30 mins**   *Cooking time:* **10 mins**

tab tim grob
red rubies

handful jasmine flowers
150ml water
150g palm sugar
350ml coconut milk
150g water chestnuts
200g tapioca flour
1 tbsp red food colouring
crushed ice
1.5 litres water

To make jasmine essence, soak the jasmine flowers in 150ml water, covered, overnight.

To make the syrup, place the jasmine essence, palm sugar and coconut milk in a pan, bring to the boil then remove from the heat and leave to cool.

Slice the water chestnuts into cubes and place in a bowl with the red food colouring. Stir together until the water chestnuts are bright red.

Put the flour on a plate and add the water chestnuts, stirring together so the pieces are well-coated. Place in a strainer and shake to remove the excess flour.

Bring the 1.5 litres of water to the boil in a pan and add the water chestnuts. Cook until they float which means they are ready. Remove, drain and plunge into cold water immediately.

Divide the water chestnuts between four dessert dishes, add the syrup and fill with crushed ice.

Serves: **4**   *Prep time:* **20 mins**   *Cooking time:* **10 mins**

Wine with food, at Khams

Dispelling the myth that wine and Asian food are not a good match, Kham Signavong is well-known in Australian and New Zealand wine circles (and beyond!) for his discerning palate and very fine wine cellar.

"Cool climate wines are a perfect match."

Naturally my recommendations apply to my own cuisine. People who love the often overly-sweet tastes of the Central Thai food served in some restaurants or come to know Thai food that is not properly balanced would not necessarily find my suggestions suitable. However my discerning clients who know good wine love to taste new vintages, discoveries and limited releases that I am able to source.

Why cool climate?

It is well-known that wines with good acidity are a good food match and those with moderate acidity made from cool climate fruit are the best of all. Some white and rosé wines also fall into this category.

Wines low in acidity can't compete with the salty and sour flavours in Asian food while dry wines without any sweetness at all can't complement the sweet notes which are integral to balanced Thai cooking. Interestingly, peppery wines high in alcohol content do not necessarily complement very spicy food.

Red wines generally need to be high in fruit and with moderate alcohol and tannin levels to balance spicy, salty flavours – and then the whole food-matching process goes from there with individual wines and vintages pairing with certain dishes.

Many of my favourite wines come from wine-makers who nurture their vineyards and their grapes in the same way that we approach our cooking. My friends at Howard Park in West Australia's Margaret River work to produce high quality wines which are good value. The Howard Park Riesling goes beautifully with, say, Thai lobster, steamed fish and scallops, while the Howard Park Shiraz goes well with Isan food including dishes such as Crying Tiger, duck salad, goat curry and dishes which are rich but not too chilli-hot.

In South Australia's McLaren Vale, my friends at Dowie Doole produce a Chenin Blanc noted for citrusy and green fruit flavours making it a great match with seafood including oyster and scallop dishes, salads and some chicken. Dowie Doole Cabernet Sauvignon has lovely cassis and cigar box notes and generous fruit going well with lamb, beef and heavier dishes such as Gaeng Hang Lay.

"Many of my favourite wines come from wine-makers who nurture their vineyards and their grapes the same way that we approach our cooking."

Lime juice, granite and floral notes hinting of apple blossom and jasmine.

The intense lime fruit characters drive through the finish which is tightly wound yet lingering with floral and wet stone hints. This wine has been made with an eye to cellaring.

Basket-pressed fruits with underlying Dutch liquorice and five spice.

It displays lifted intense blackberry and dark plum fruit aromas and spices: traces of cinnamon, cloves and anise evolve as the wine opens up. Complemented by dark chocolate and mocha complexity which will develop with further cellaring.

Ripe, sweet berries, dark chocolate and blackcurrants.

The palate is rich and full, featuring long, savoury and dark-berried flavours and cabernet choc-mint characters. The oak is very well integrated leaving the wine with a soft, rounded tannin finish.

Almost water white with pale straw hues.

Beautiful, lively aromas of tropical fruits and melon with hints of honeysuckle on the nose. The palate exhibits excellent fruit intensity of tropical, citrus and green fruit flavours followed by zesty acidity. The mouth-feel is crisp, clean and refreshing.

Ripe black cherry, spice box with roast meat and gamey aromas.

A mouthful of rich, black cherries and blackberries, earth, tar and dark chocolate characters on a warm, full-bodied palate. Quite firm tannins and fine acidity will soften with age and ensure that this wine will drink extremely well over the next 5–10 years.

"My personal selection includes wines such as these which I choose to complement my food."

Pastes and Sauces

What would Thai food be without its pastes and sauces?
Many recipes in Khun's Sai Mae Nam call for pastes
that are particular to a dish, while others are generic such
as red, green, yellow and roasted chilli pastes.

You will see that I always recommend using a pestle and mortar to crush the herbs to release their rich range of juices and combine them in a way that cannot be achieved as effectively using a blender or food processor.

Some ingredients can be chopped up using a food processor first, while dry ingredients such as peppercorns and coriander seeds can be ground in a coffee grinder you might keep for the purpose if you cook a lot of Thai food.

Pounding is a skill handed down through the generations and good cooks are experts at blending their herbs and spices in this fashion.

Time-poor cooks will reach for ready-made curry pastes and you can do this, of course, but I recommend that you find varieties that are not too sweet. If you like to cook Thai food often, make larger quantities of curry pastes to keep in the fridge for up to 3 months.

nam prik chu chee *chu chee paste*

8 dried chillies

3 tbsp finely sliced garlic

2 tbsp finely sliced shallot

1 tsp salt

1 tsp shrimp paste

2 tbsp finely sliced lemongrass

1 tbsp finely sliced galangal

1 tsp finely sliced kaffir lime rind

1 tsp peppercorns

Soak the dried chillies in warm water for 30 minutes then remove and de-seed. Add the chillies to the remaining ingredients and pound together to a fine paste.

nam prik gaeng pu
seafood curry paste

1 tbsp coriander seeds

½ tsp cumin seeds

3 big green chillies, finely chopped

15 hot green chillies, finely chopped

2 tbsp finely chopped garlic

4 tbsp finely chopped shallot

1 tbsp finely chopped lemongrass

1 tbsp finely chopped coriander root

1 tbsp finely chopped kaffir lime rind

½ tbsp finely chopped galangal

1 tbsp finely chopped fresh turmeric
(or ½ tbsp turmeric powder)

1 tsp salt

1 tbsp shrimp paste

Wrap the shrimp paste in a banana leaf or foil and grill for 5 minutes to aromatise. Toast the coriander and cumin seeds in a dry wok until the seeds have browned. Remove and pound them with the shrimp paste and remaining ingredients to a fine paste.

234

nam prik gaeng kua *gaeng kua paste*

15 large dried chillies
1 tbsp finely chopped galangal
1 tbsp finely chopped lemongrass
1 tsp sea salt
4 tbsp finely chopped shallot
4 tbsp finely chopped garlic
½ tbsp kaffir lime rind
2 coriander roots
1 tbsp shrimp paste

Soak the dried chillies in warm water for ½ hour then remove and de-seed. Pound the chilli with the galangal, lemongrass and salt to a fine paste then slowly add all remaining ingredients while continuing to pound to a fine paste.

nam prik gaeng som *gaeng som chilli paste*

10 hot red chillies
2 tbsp finely chopped garlic
1 tbsp lesser ginger (krachai), finely chopped
2 tbsp shallots, finely chopped
1 tsp salt
1 tbsp shrimp paste

Pound the chillies, garlic, lesser ginger, shallots and salt to a fine paste. Add the shrimp paste and mix well.

nam prik gaeng khao wan *green curry paste*

1 tsp coriander seeds
½ tsp cumin seeds
10 green bird's eye chillies, or long green chillies, chopped
1 tbsp finely sliced lemongrass
3 tbsp chopped shallot
1 tsp sliced galangal
1 tsp chopped coriander root
1 tbsp ground black pepper
½ tsp grated kaffir lime zest
1 tsp shrimp paste
5 tbsp chopped garlic
1 tsp salt

Toast the coriander and cumin seeds in a wok, then grind them until fine using a pestle and mortar. Add the remaining ingredients and pound to a fine paste

nam prik gaeng hang lay *gaeng hang lay paste*

1 tbsp shrimp paste

4 garlic cloves, unpeeled

5 shallots, unpeeled

1 tbsp finely sliced lemongrass

1 tbsp coriander seeds

1 tbsp cumin seeds

5 large dried chillies

1 tsp turmeric powder

½ tsp salt

Soak the dried chillies in warm water for 30 minutes, then remove and de-seed. Heat the oven to 160°C, wrap the shrimp paste in foil and place it with the garlic and shallots on a baking tray and bake for 10 minutes. Remove form the over and cool, then peel off the skins. Fry the coriander and cumin seeds in a wok until golden brown and aromatised. Now pound all the ingredients together to a fine paste.

nam prik khao soi *khao soi chilli paste*

5 dried bird's eye chillies

1½ tbsp peeled andf sliced shallot

2 tbsp chopped garlic

1 tbsp chopped lemongrass

½ tbsp galangal

1 tsp grated kaffir lime zest

½ tsp ground turmeric

1 tsp coriander seeds

Soak the dried chillies in warn water for 30 minutes then remove and de-seed. Now pound the chillies and remaining ingredients together to a fine paste.

nam prik khua kling (tai pla)
khua kling curry paste

15 hot chillies

15 dried birdseye chillies

1 tbsp finely chopped galangal

1 tbsp finely chopped lemongrass

2 tsp salt

1 tbsp shrimp paste

1 tbsp finely chopped fresh turmeric (or ½ tbsp turmeric powder)

3 tbsp finely chopped shallot

3 tbsp finely chopped garlic

½ tbsp finely chopped coriander root

Soak the dried chillies in warm water for 30 minutes, then remove and de-seed. Pound all the ingredients to a fine paste.

nam prik larb khua
larb khua paste

1 tbsp coriander seeds

1 cardamom pod

½ tsp nutmeg

1 cinnamon stick cut in half

½ tsp ground mace

½ tbsp black peppercorns

1 tbsp Sichuan peppercorns

2 tbsp chopped shallots

15 dried hot chillies

5 big chilli peppers

½ tbsp galangal rings

½ tsp chopped garlic

Heat a large pan and dry-fry the coriander seeds, cardamom, nutmeg, cinnamon, ground mace and peppercorns until aromatised and golden brown. Remove from the pan and set aside.

Pound the shallots, chillies, galangal and shrimp paste together using a pestle and mortar, add the dry spices and mix well.

nam prik gaeng panang
panang curry paste

1 tbsp shrimp paste

½ tbsp black peppercorns

3 tbsp coriander seeds

½ tbsp cumin seeds

15 large dried red chillies

2 tbsp chopped shallots

1 tbsp finely sliced lemongrass

4 sliced galangal ringss

2 tbsp chopped coriander root

3 tbsp crushed toasted mung beans

4 tbsp chopped garlic

Wrap the shrimp paste in foil and grill for 5 minutes to aromatise. Toast the dry seeds in a wok until golden brown, then pound all the ingredients together to a fine paste.

pad prik khing
prik khing chilli paste

part a:

5 large dried chillies

1 tsp coriander seeds

1 tsp cardamom seeds

1 tsp cumin seeds

1 tsp galangal

1 tbsp finely chopped lemongrass

2 tbsp chopped garlic

2 tbsp chopped shallot

1 tsp salt

1 tbsp shrimp paste

part b:

4 kaffir lime leaves, finely sliced

2 tsp cooking oil

2 tsp fish sauce

½ tbsp sugar

2 tsp dried shrimp, roughly blended

Soak the dried chillies in warm water for 30 minutes, then remove and de-seed. Toast the coriander, cardamom and cumin seeds in a wok over a medium heat until golden brown. Pound all the remaining ingredients for part a to a fine paste then add kaffir lime leaves. Heat the oil in a wok and fry the paste until it thickens, then season with fish sauce and sugar.

nam prik gaeng phet
red curry paste

1 tbsp shrimp paste

1tbsp coriander seeds

½ tsp cumin seeds

15 large dried chillies

1 stem lemongrass, finely sliced

2 tbsp chopped shallot

1 tbsp minced garlic

1 tbsp grated galangal

1 tbsp freshly ground black pepper

1 coriander root, chopped

½ tsp kaffir lime zest, finely chopped

1 tsp salt

Soak the dried chillies in warm water for 30 minutes, remove and de-seed. Wrap the shrimp paste in foil and grill for 5 minutes to aromatise. Toast the coriander and cumin seeds in a wok, then pound them until fine using a pestle and mortar, then add the remaining ingredients and pound to a fine paste.

nam prik pao
roasted chilli paste

5 dried red chillies

4 tbsp vegetable oil

3 tbsp chopped garlic

1 tbsp chopped shallot

1 tbsp shrimp paste

1 tbsp palm sugar

1 tbsp tamarind juice
(see page 242)

1½ tsp salt

Soak the dried chillies in warm water for 30 minutes, then remove and de-seed. Heat the oil in a wok over a medium heat and fry the garlic and shallot until golden brown then remove and set aside. Now fry the chillies until brown, then remove and pound them with the fried garlic, shallot and shrimp paste until fine. Return the mix to the wok and add palm sugar, tamarind juice and salt and stir-fry until the mixture aromatises and thickens.

nam prik gaeng kari
yellow curry paste

12 dried chillies

1 tbsp coriander seeds

1 tsp cumin seeds

½ tsp ground cinnamon

1 tsp sea salt

2 tbsp thickly sliced shallot

4 tbsp chopped garlic

1 tbsp thickly sliced galangal

2 tbsp sliced lemongrass

2 tbsp thickly sliced fresh turmeric

2 tsp curry powder

1 tsp shrimp paste

1 tbsp finely chopped ginger

Soak the dried chillies in warm water for 30 minutes, then remove from the water and de-seed. Dry-fry the coriander seed and cumin seeds over a medium heat fry until browned and aromatised. Pound all the ingredients to a fine paste.

garlic oil

5 tbsp oil

3 tbsp roughly chopped garlic

Heat the oil, add the garlic and cook until golden, stirring frequently to make sure it doesn't burn. Allow to cool, then store in a tightly sealed glass jar or bottle until ready to use in Get Well Soon Soup, noodles and steamed fish dishes.

jiew pla ra
spicy anchovy dipping sauce

5 shallots, unpeeled

10 cloves garlic, unpeeled

20 hot chillies

5 rings galangal

3 tbsp anchovy sauce

2 tbsp lemon juice

2 tbsp fish sauce

2 tbsp sugar

2 stems lemongrass

handful kaffir lime leaves. finely chopped

Grill the shallots, garlic, chillies and galangal for about 5 minutes, or until brown. Remove from the heat, cool and peel then pound together using a pestle and mortar. Heat the anchovy sauce in a small pan for about 3–4 minutes, slowly adding the paste, lemon juice, fish sauce, kaffir lime leaves and sugar, to season.

khao yam sauce

250ml water

2 tbsp preserved fish (nam budu)

2 tbsp ground palm sugar

2 tbsp ground galangal

4 shallots, peeled and finely chopped

1 stem lemongrass, chopped into 75-mm pieces

10 kaffir lime leaves, torn

1 tbsp fish sauce

Boil the water in small pan then add the remaining ingredients. Boil for 5 minutes, stirring, then simmer gently for 40 minutes, stirring from time to time, until the sauce thickens. Filter the sauce through a fine mesh strainer.

nam jim ajar cucumber relish

225ml water

100g caster sugar

125ml white wine vinegar

pinch of salt

1 cucumber, sliced and slices quartered

1 shallot, peeled and finely sliced

2 small red chillies, finely chopped

4 coriander leaves for garnish

Boil the water in a amll pan then add the sugar and stir until it has dissolved. Add the vinegar and salt, then remove from the heat and cool. When ready to serve, add the cucumber, shallot and chilli and top with coriander.

nam jim jiew *isan chilli sauce*

2 tsp chilli powder

2 tsp ground roasted rice

½ tsp caster sugar

2 tbsp fresh lime juice

1 tbsp fish sauce

2 tbsp light soy sauce

1 tsp chopped coriander leaves

1 tsp chopped shallot

Mix the chilli powder, rice, sugar, lime juice, fish sauce and soy together in a bowl until the sugar has dissolved. Add coriander and shallot when ready to serve.

nam jim talay
seafood dipping sauce

8–10 chillies, to taste

3 cloves garlic chopped

2 coriander roots

3 tbsp fish sauce

3 tbsp lime juice

1 tsp finely chopped coriander leaves

3 tsp sugar

Use a pestle and mortar to pound the chilli, garlic and coriander root to a paste. In a bowl combine the fish sauce, lime juice and sugar, stirring until the sugar has dissolved. Now add the paste, mix well and add the coriander leaves.

nam jim satay *satay sauce*

400ml coconut milk

½ tbsp Red Curry Paste (see page 238)

125g crushed roasted peanuts

½ tbsp salt to taste

3 tbsp sugar to taste

Heat 100 ml coconut milk in a pan, add the red curry paste stir mixing well until the red curry is separating from the coconut milk then add the remaining coconut milk. When boiling, add the crushed peanuts and stir to mix. Lower the heat, add sugar and salt to taste and continue to stir to prevent burning.

si racha prik *prik sauce*

10 red chillies

10 cloves garlic, peeled

1 tablespoon white vinegar

1 tsp salt

1 tsp caster sugar

½ tablespoon water

Blend all the ingredients together in a blender for about 5 minutes.

tamarind sauce

1tbsp oil

1 clove garlic, peeled and finely chopped

2 tbsp palm sugar

150ml water

4 tbsp tamarind juice

1 big red chilli, finely chopped

1-1½ tsp salt

2 tsp cornflour dissolved in 2 tbsp water

Heat the oil in a pan, add the garlic and cook, stirring, until golden brown. Add the palm sugar, water, tamarind juice, chilli and salt and stir well. Bring to the boil, slowly add the cornflour mix and stir until the sauce thickens.

241

methods & ingredients

coconut milk and cream

Some recipes call for an amount of coconut cream to be heated with curry paste before adding the remainder of the coconut milk. For Thais it is second nature to use the coconut cream from the top of the coconut milk - just remember not to shake the can before you open it!

pounding

The correct way to pound with a pestle and mortar is to be constant and quick. In Thailand the technique is passed on in the family from the mother-in-law and Thais can tell by the sound and rhythm of the pounding whether the person doing it is a good cook or not.

Tip: Add a little water if the ingredients being pounded are not forming a wet enough paste.

sticky rice

Sticky or glutinous rice is eaten in Northern Thailand, Isan and Laos. It is soaked overnight before cooking by steaming or in a rice cooker.

250g sticky rice

1.5 litres water

Rinse the sticky rice and soak in cold water overnight. Rinse again and place in a bamboo basket steamer to steam over boiling water for 15-20 minutes. (Or line a stainless steel steamer with cloth to steam the rice.)

As soon as the rice is cooked, ladle it out onto a flat surface and press with a wooden spoon to release the steam and moisture. The rice should stick to itself but not your fingers.

pickled garlic

Thais use garlic pickled in vinegar and sugar as a sauce for some dishes and as a condiment to add to taste. You can buy it in jars or make your own.

sawtooth leaves

These leaves are quite similar in taste to coriander and have serrated leaves (hence sawtooth) and a lovely aroma.

shrimp paste

Made from fermented shrimp, this paste is used throughout Thailand. Some recipes call for shrimp paste to be grilled or heated prior to use which helps to release the flavours.

tamarind juice

Although tamarind concentrate is available, freshly made tamarind juice is the best for Thai cooking as it is more intense in flavour. Make your own tamarind juice by soaking 1/3 block tamarind pulp in a litre of warm water, then squeezing the pulp with your hands and then straining through a sieve to separate the juice.

toasted ground dried chilli

Dried chillies are finely ground using a pestle and mortar or an electric grinder and dry-toasted in a wok.

toasted ground rice

Ground rice is dry-toasted in a wok until golden brown.

vinegar chillies

De-seeded green chillies pickled in vinegar with salt added to taste.

For more information go to: www.arunthai.com.au

index

244

acknowledgements

without heart we are nothing

Writing things down has never been a Thai tradition. We react to the influences of the day and make our decisions accordingly – even our recipes change slightly from day to day depending on the produce available and fine details such as the heat of the chillies and the freshness of the produce. I think the world is slowly returning to that way of thinking with use of fresh seasonal produce and certainly my suppliers in Australia provide a wonderful choice with quality which is second to none.

I would like to thank all those who have helped to make the book possible including my friends and customers who have encouraged and inspired me along the way, my staff and, of course, my parents, my lovely wife Tess and my wonderful children Khristopher and Katherine.

The team that produced this book was very small, essentially just four of us (seen opposite, top, in Mae Hon Song, l-r: Peter Metro, myself, Ken Martin, Alison Plummer). We wanted to create something from our hearts and, naturally, the project grew by the week.

My long-time friend, photographer Ken Martin took the beautiful photographs and directed the project working on the concept with our friend, talented designer Peter Metro whose expert crafting and eye for detail help make this book so very special.

Publishing editor Alison Plummer interpreted the recipes, brought her own eye to photo shoots and patiently tackled the challenge of Thai history as well as Thai name interpretations, which she describes as 'flexible at best'! Our thanks to Michelle Metro and the editorial team for the patient rounds of proof-reading, also to Max and to Charlie for assistance with the index.

On one of our trips to Thailand this year we travelled for nearly three weeks to photograph and film (our DVD will available in 2010), meeting wonderful people along the way. Our thanks to all those who made us so welcome and shared their recipes and hospitality. Special thanks to my family in Thailand, especially my uncles Yin and Channat and their familes, Uncle Tynoi and all at United Production Press.

My thanks to Thai Airways, Thai Trade/Thai Select and Thai Tourism and to Chang Beer, especially Lesley Lee, for supporting our project. Also thanks to my associates in the wine trade – especially Howard Park and Dowie Doole for their generous support and friendship.

Kham

Khamtane Signavong, September 9, 2009

www.arunthai.com.au

special thanks

Thai Trade and Thai Select
www.thaiselect.com.au

Thai Airways
www.thaiairways.com.au www.thaiairways.com

Thai Tourism, especially Pongsak Kanittanon.
www.tourismthailand.org

Chang Beer www.changbeer.com

Howard Park Wines www.howardparkwines.com.au

Dowie Doole www.dowiedoole.com.au

Images: © Ken Martin/True Blue Cockatoo www.bluecockatoo.com.au

Additional photography: © Peter Metro & Alison Plummer
Cave paintings & river scene, page 64; Rice Barges at Ayutthaya, page 157;
Royal Barge on the Chao Phraya River, page 183;
reproduced courtesy of Thai Tourism. www.thailand.net.au

Dishes pages 29, 105, 217 from a range by Fink Design www.finkdesign.com

Glassware, pages 125, 127, Spiegelau Glass. Tel: 02 9966 0033